DEDICATION

This book is dedicated
to you, and all aspiring artists!

Happy Drawing!

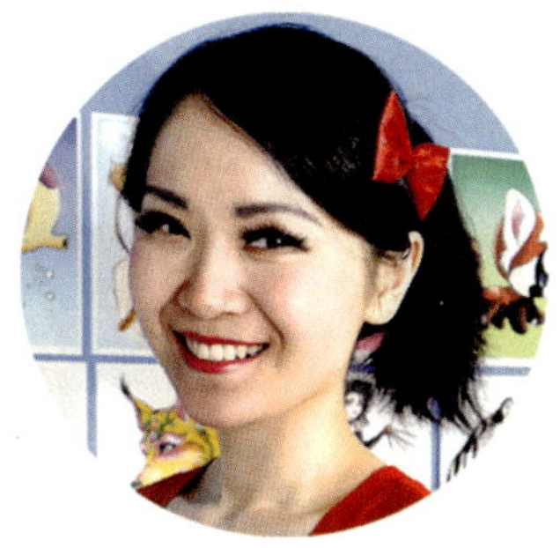

COPYRIGHT

Published by Mei Yu Art Inc.

Paperback ISBN: 978-1-990391-46-0
eBook ISBN: 978-1-989939-28-4
First Published October 2021
Book design, cover design, and illustrations by Mei Yu.

For business inquiries, please contact Mei Yu.

BY MEI YU

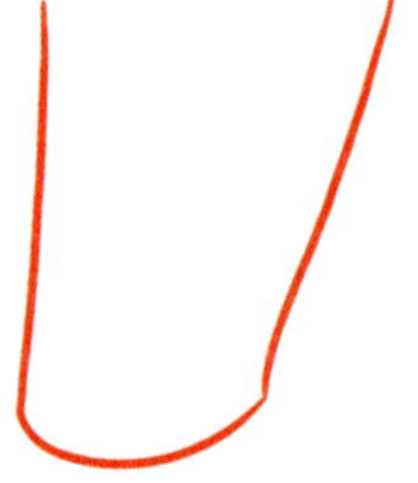

1.
Start with the ankle tapered in.

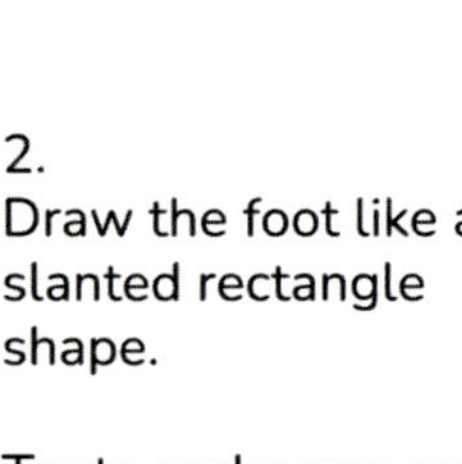

2.
Draw the foot like a slanted rectangle shape.

Try to make one corner larger for the heel.

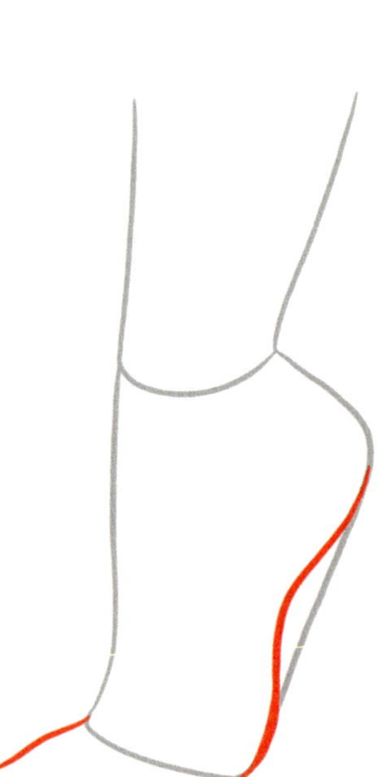

3.
Draw curved lines to show the arch in the foot. Make a general shape for the toes first.

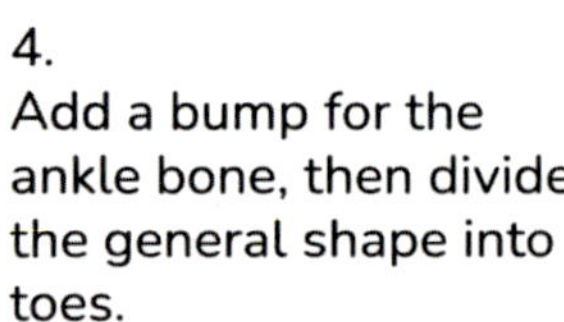

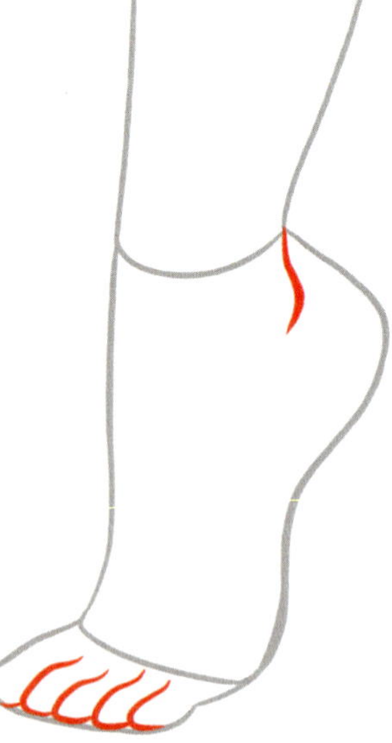

4.
Add a bump for the ankle bone, then divide the general shape into toes.

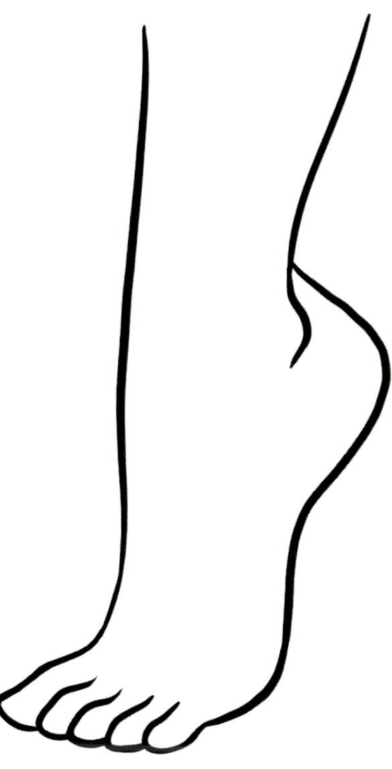

5.
Erase extra lines and finalize your drawing! Use your choice of a black marker, pen, or brush pen.

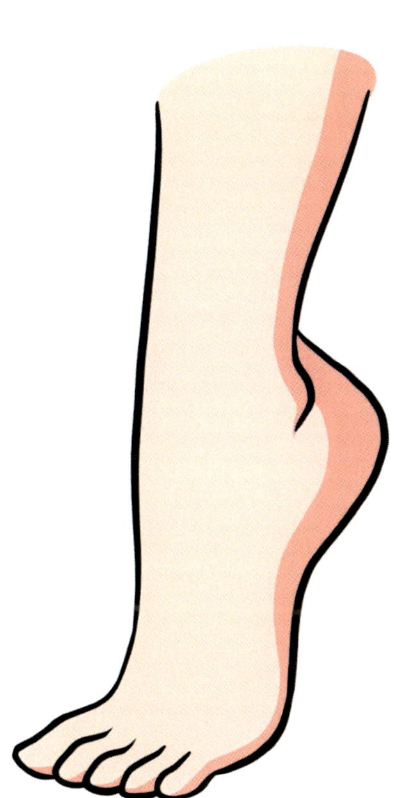

This is an elegant pose for a character who might be relaxing on the sofa, or standing on her toes.

Try drawing the other pretty poses for feet in this book to enhance your own characters! The ***more*** you draw, the ***better*** you draw!

BY MEI YU

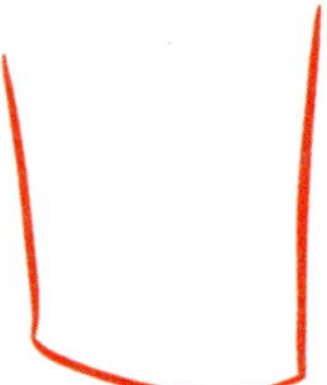

1.
Begin with the ankle. The lines aren't exactly parallel - they taper slightly at the bottom for a natural look.

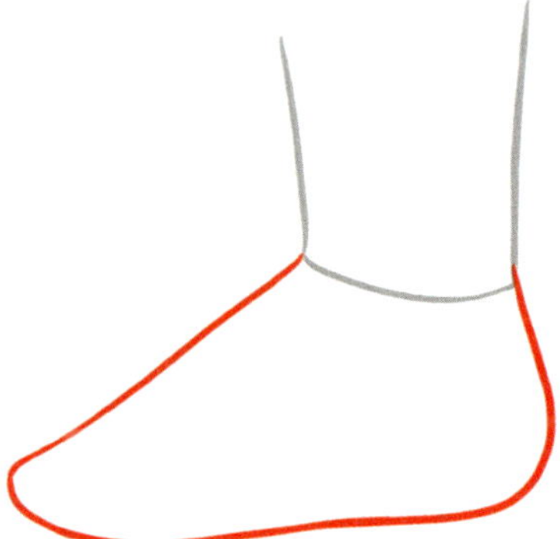

2.
Start the foot with a rounded triangle. The heel part is wide, curved, and soft.

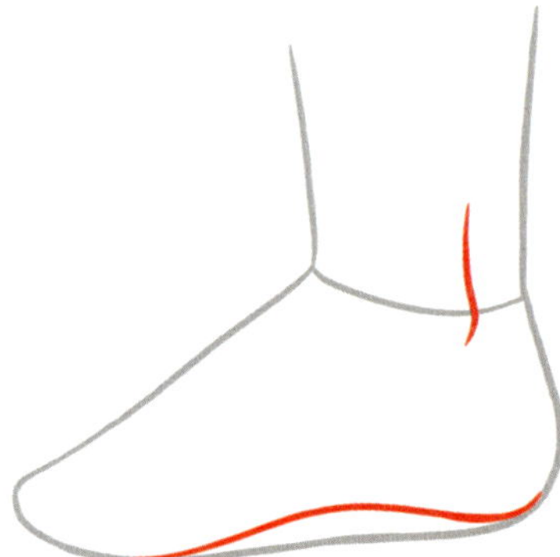

3.
Draw the arch of the foot, and then the ankle bone.

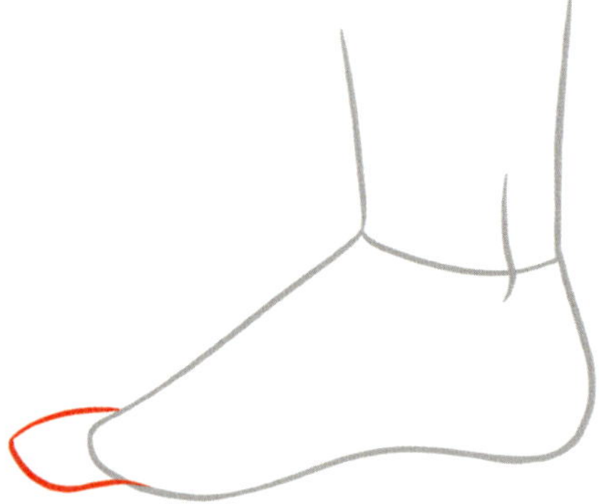

4.
Add a small curved shape for the toes.

BY MEI YU

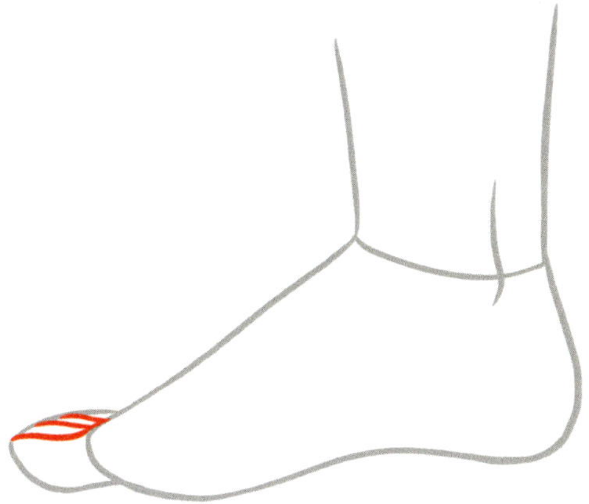

5.
Divide the shape into toes. Keep the lines close together for the perspective.

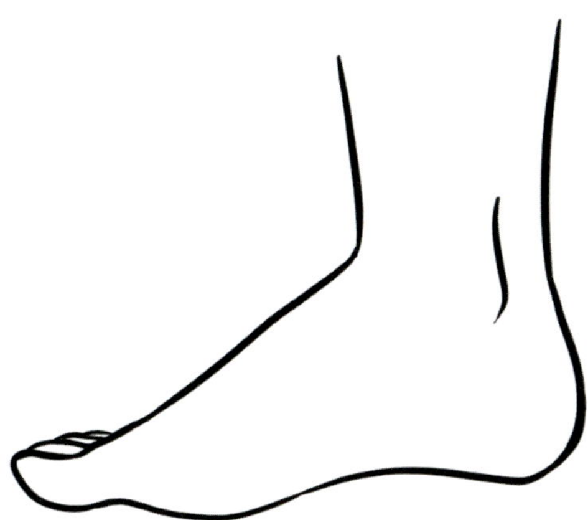

6.
Finalize your drawing!

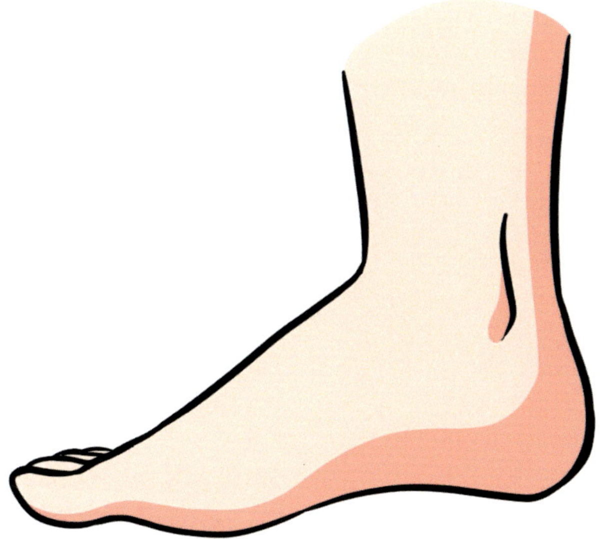

This is a good pose for a character's foot from the side. Try drawing more foot poses in the male edition of this book!

Up on Toes (from Behind)

BY MEI YU

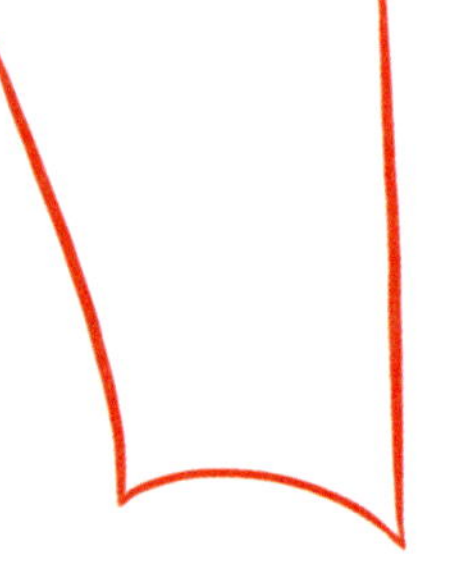

1.
Start with the ankle tapered in. Section off the ankle area with a curve to make your drawing feel more natural.

Try not to use straight or rigid lines to keep your design more organic.

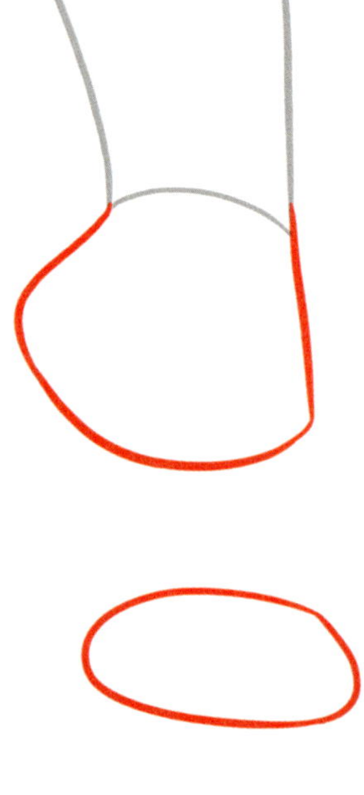

2.
Draw two round shapes with a space between them. These will be the major parts of the underside: the heel and the area where the toes bend.

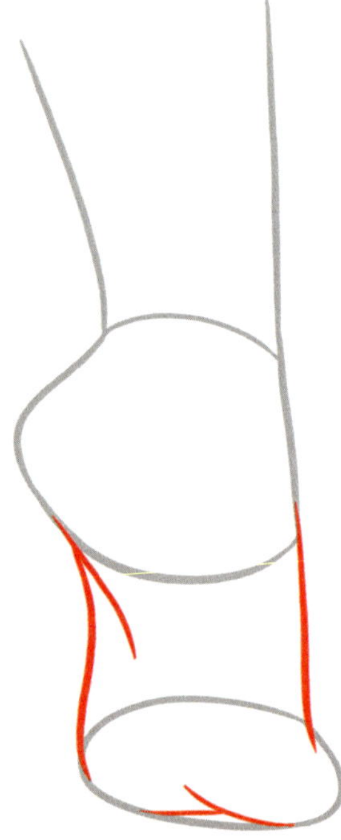

3.
Draw lines to connect the two round shapes together. Make the lines flow into the structure of the foot for a more natural look.

Up on Toes (from Behind)

4.
Add lines by the heel to show the structure of the tendon attaching to the foot. Draw a small ankle bone, then the toe.

5.
Finalize your drawing with a dark pen or black marker.

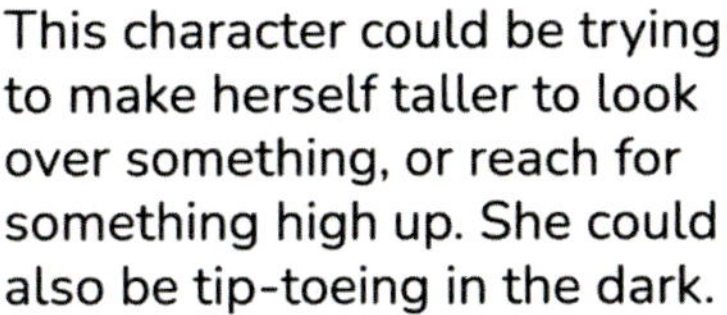

This character could be trying to make herself taller to look over something, or reach for something high up. She could also be tip-toeing in the dark.

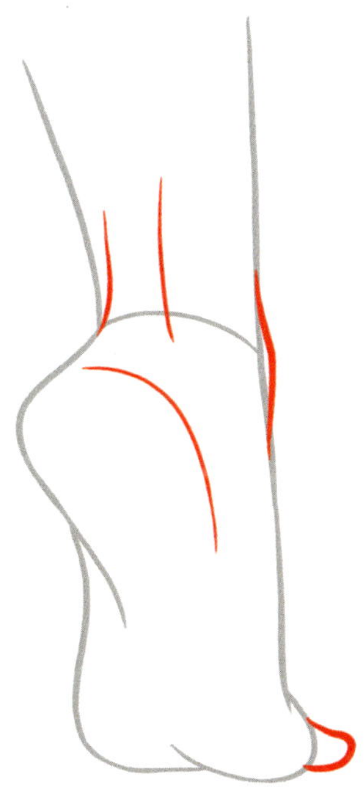

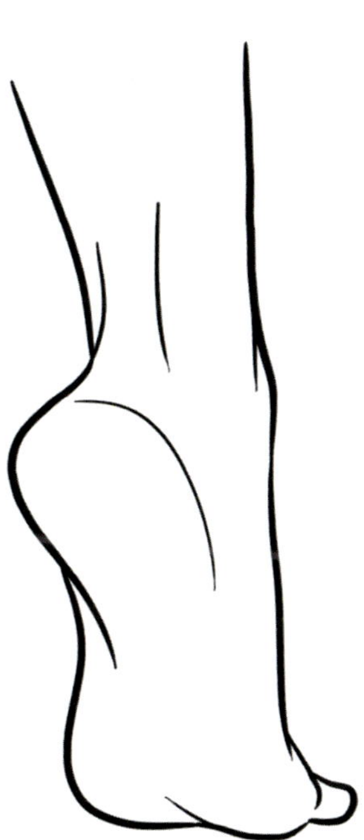

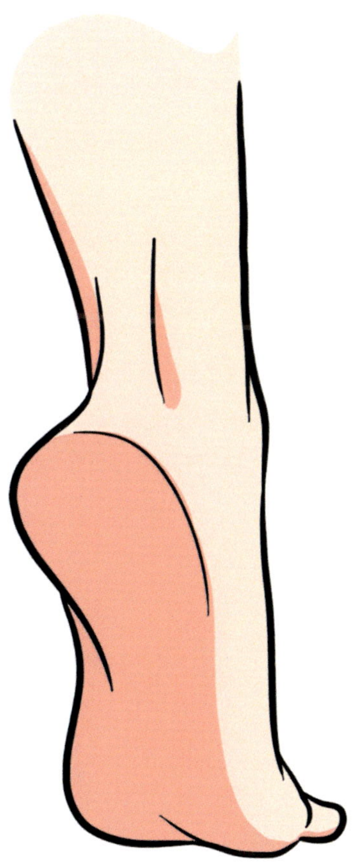

Lying Down

BY MEI YU

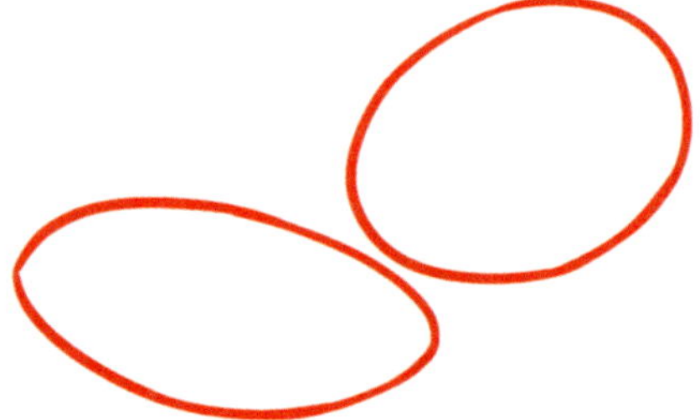

1.
Draw two ovals
to begin the foot.

2.
Connect the ovals
together. Then, add
the toe area.

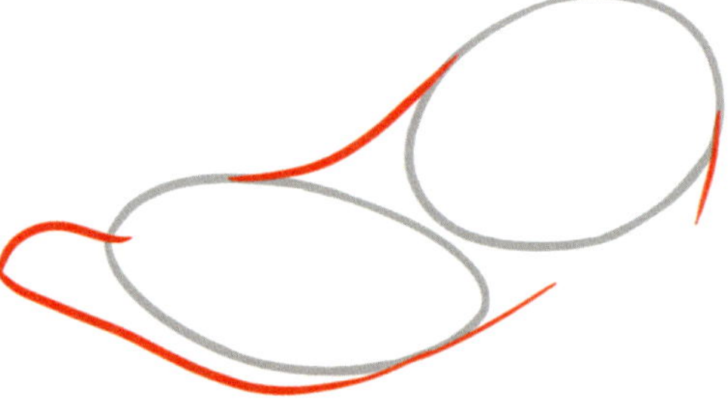

3.
Draw the ankle of the
foot, then the toes.

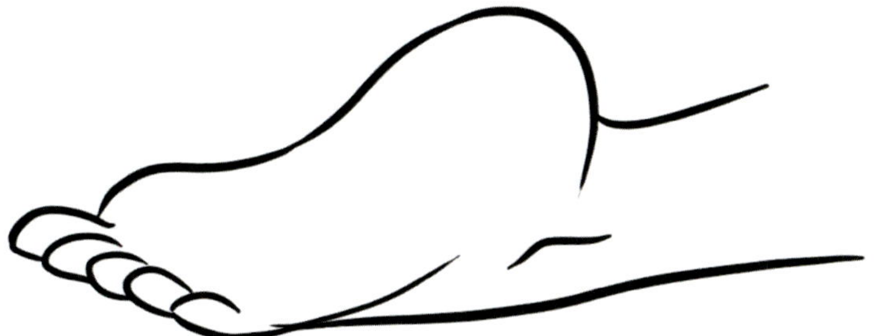

4.
Use a thin pen, brush marker, or outliner to go over the final lines. Try to make some lines thinner for a nice, graceful look.

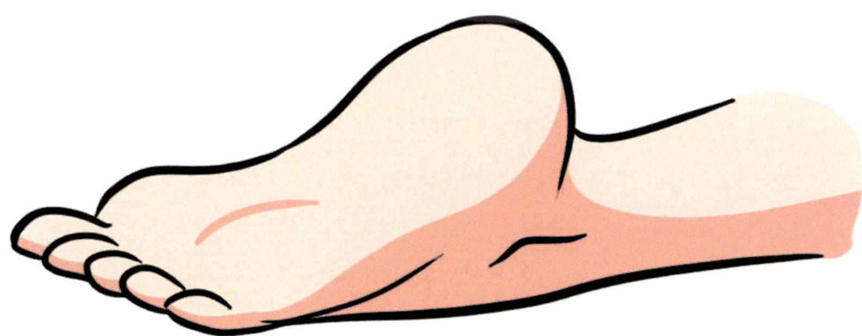

This is a good foot pose for a character who is lying down sleeping, listening to music, or diving during a baseball game!

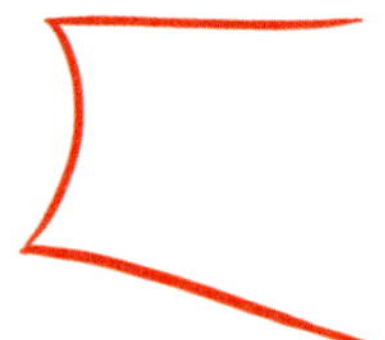

1.
Draw the ankle at a horizontal angle.

2.
Summarize the general shape of the foot as a round triangle.

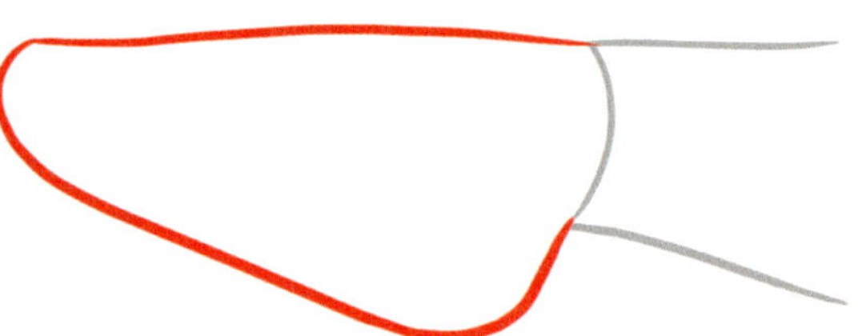

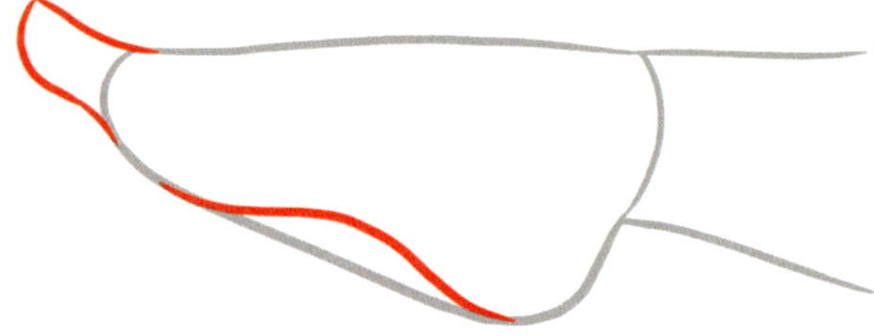

3.
Draw the curved arch for the bottom part of the foot, then add the big toe.

4.
Add the finishing details, like a few of the other toes poking out from behind the big toe.

Sometimes, it's not necessary to show all the toes in certain poses.

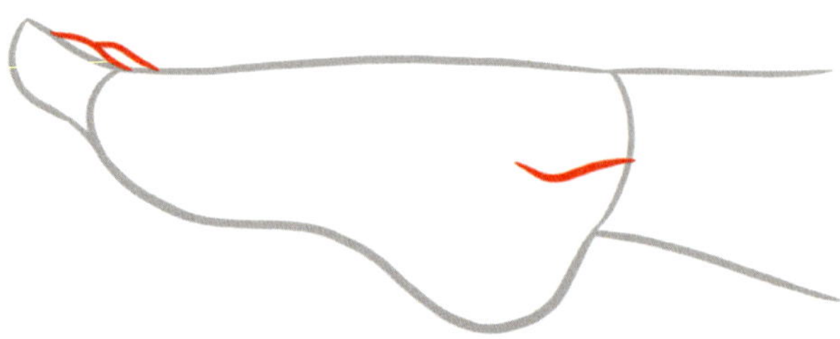

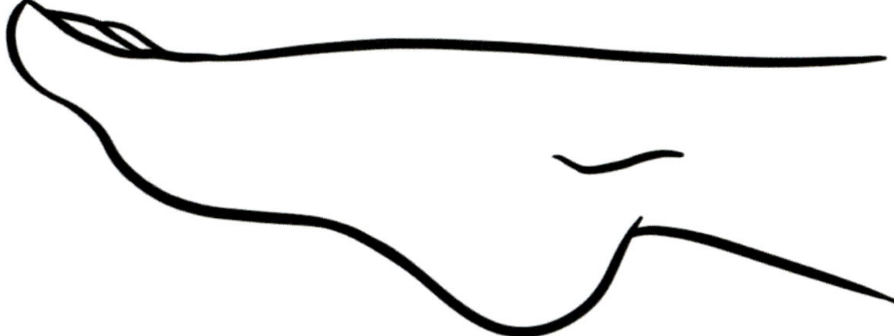

5.
Erase extra lines, then use your choice of a dark pen, marker, or outliner to go over the final lines.

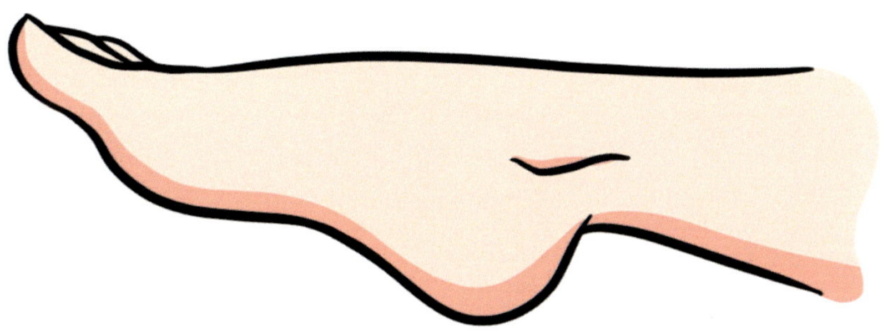

This pose can be for a character who is putting her feet up in the air, relaxing in a bathtub or spa.

She could also be doing the splits, or kicking something gently.

BY MEI YU

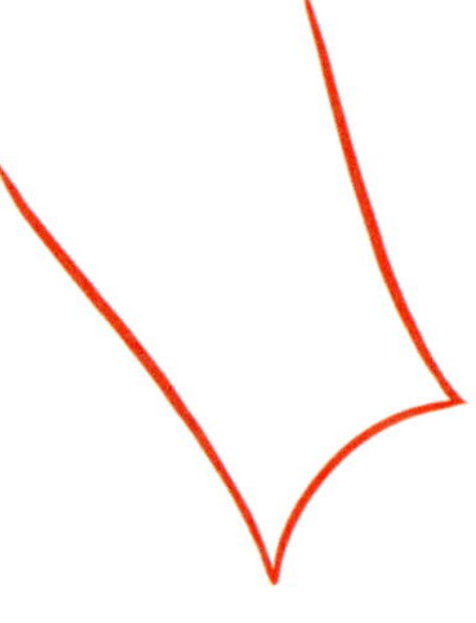

1.
Begin with the ankle area.

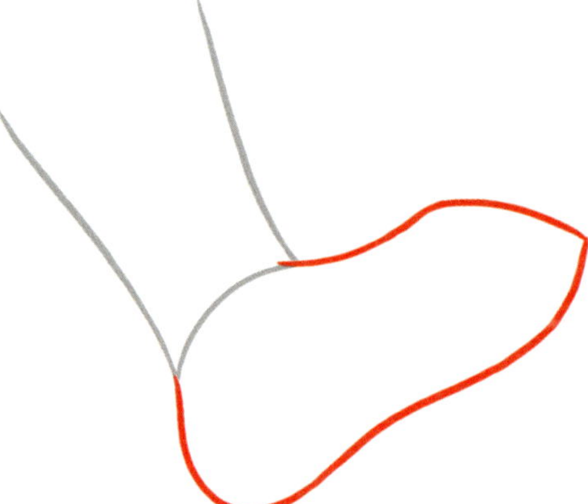

2.
Draw the foot like a rounded rectangle, with a large heel.

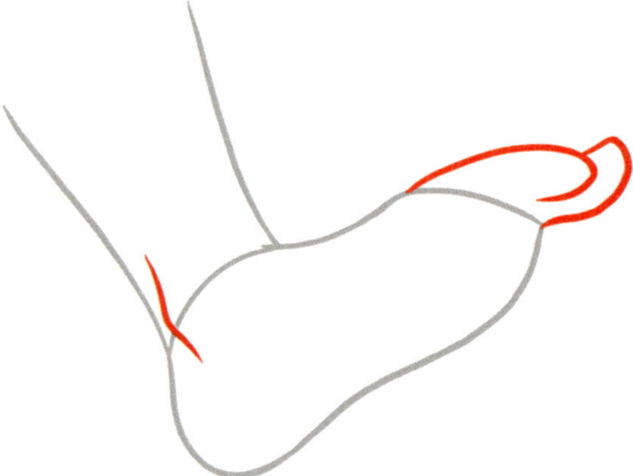

3.
Start the toes with curved lines. The big toe can angle upwards. After, draw a small bump for the ankle bone.

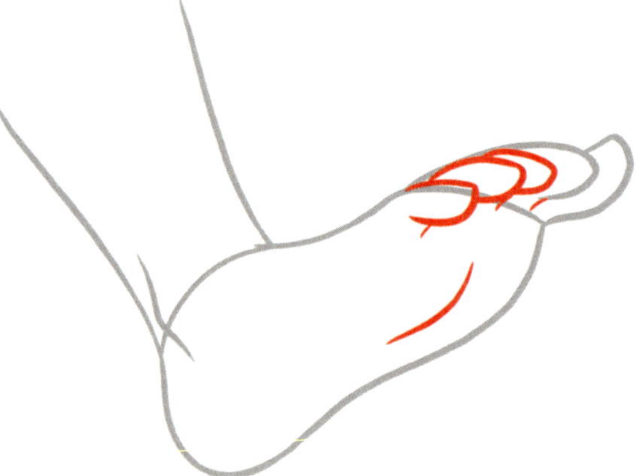

4.
Draw the rest of the toes as curves. For a graceful look, keep the toes facing the same direction.

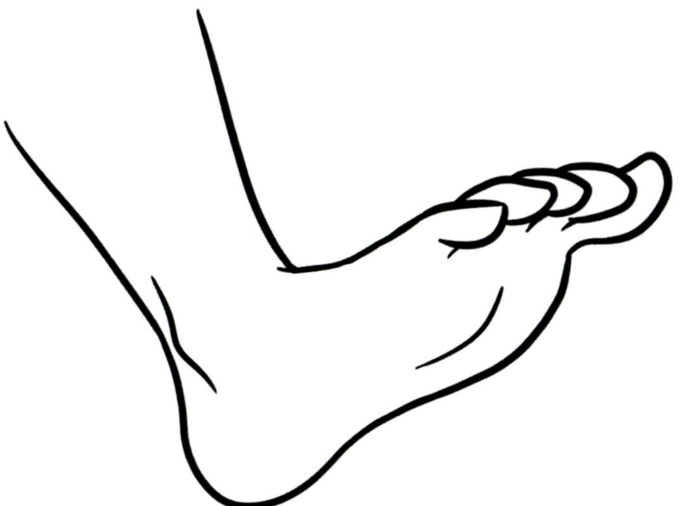

5.
Go over the final lines with a dark pen or marker.

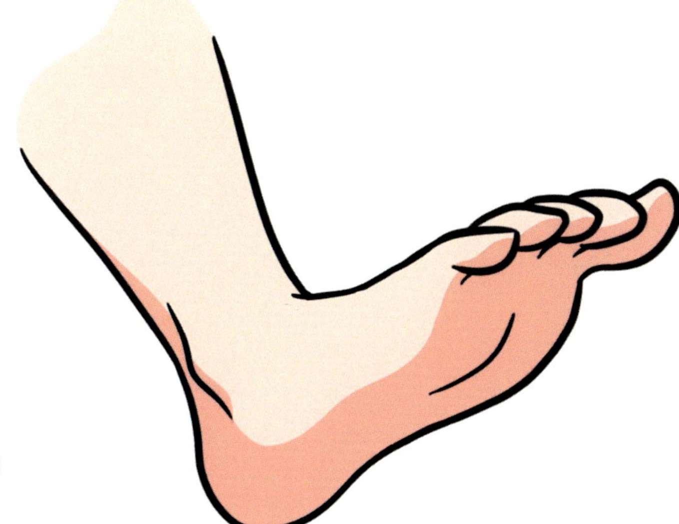

This is a great pose when a character is kicking something, like a soccer ball or a rock. She could also be kicking the ground in frustration.

BY MEI YU

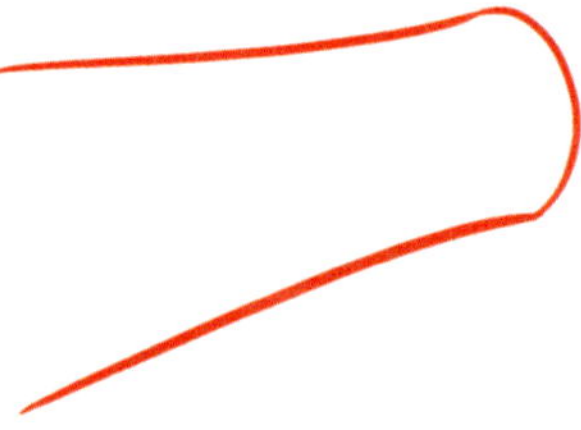

1.
Start with the lower leg tapering into the ankle.

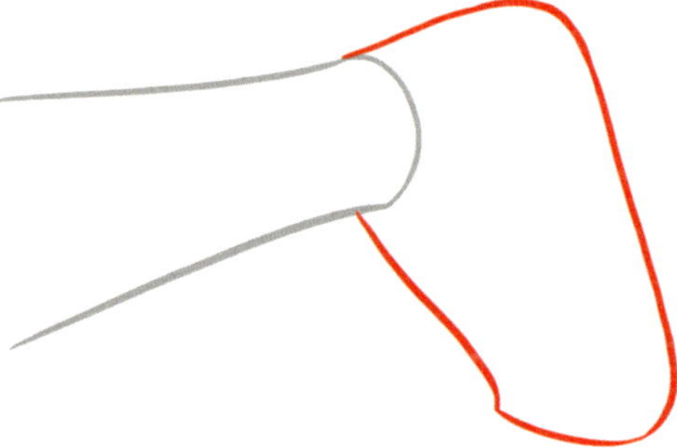

2.
Draw the foot like a rectangle shape with the heel part wider than the toe part.

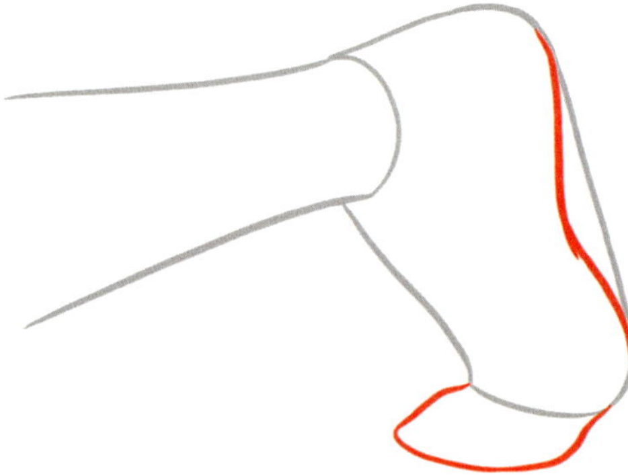

3.
Draw the arch in the foot, then the rectangle shape for the toes. For a more natural look, keep the toe shape slightly curved.

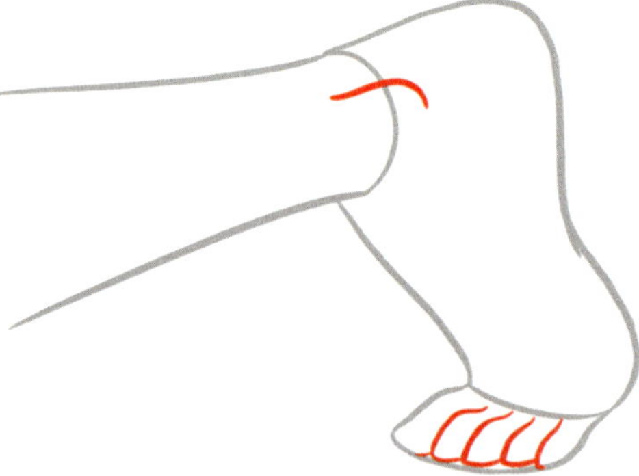

4.
Divide the toes, then add the bone bump.

BY MEI YU

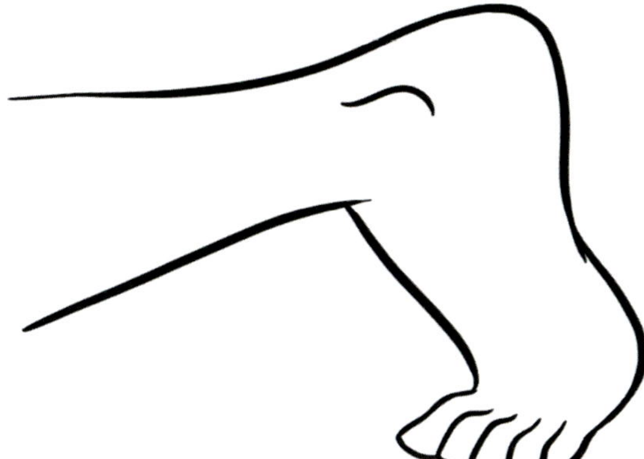

5.
Erase extra lines before going over your final drawing with a dark pen or marker.

Try this pose for a character who is pushing a heavy object on their hands and knees, or she's kneeling down to either examine something or to pick something up.

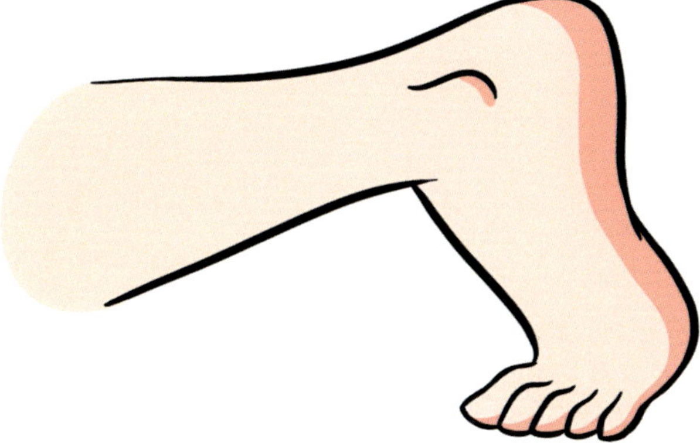

BY MEI YU

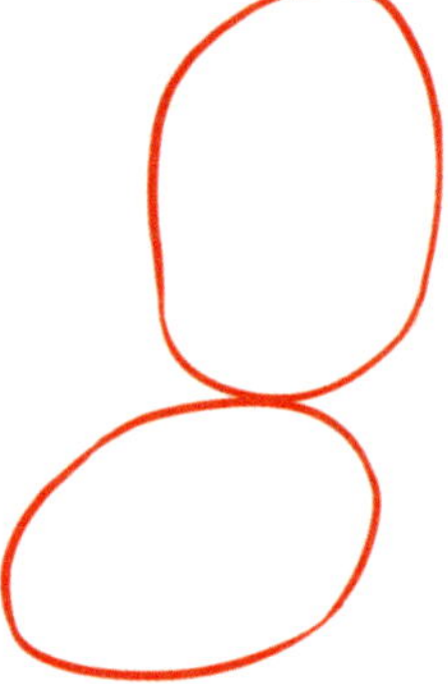

1.
Begin the foot with two round shapes.

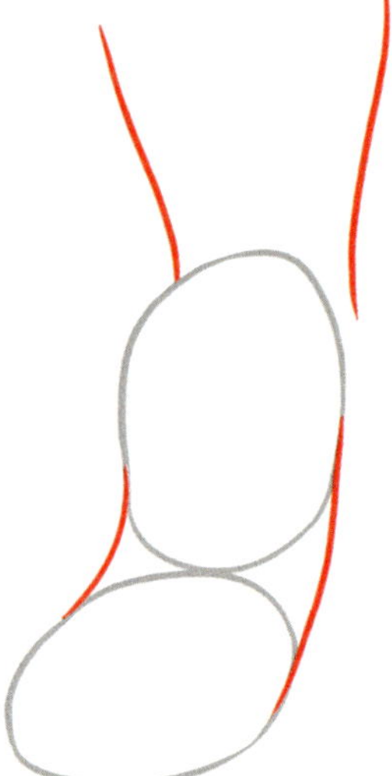

2.
Connect the two shapes with curved lines for the sides of the foot.

Then, draw part of the leg coming down to the foot. The ankle will taper in a little.

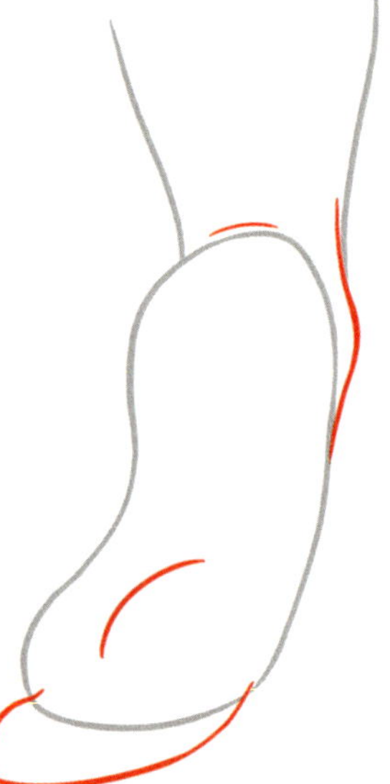

3.
Draw a curved line at the bottom to start the toe area. To show the "meaty" part of the foot, add a curve, then draw the ankle bone on the side.

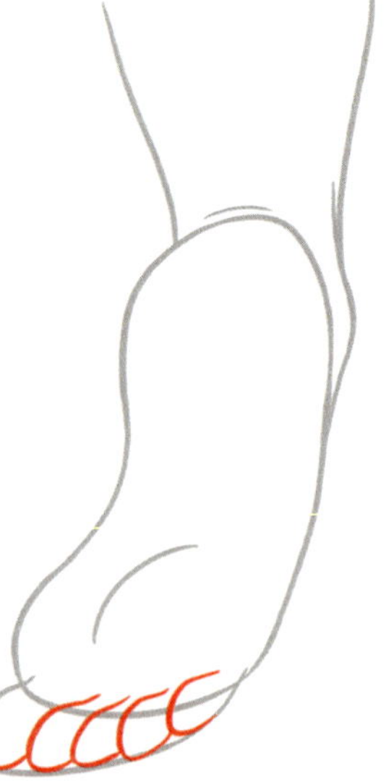

4.
Divide the toe area into individual toes - make them smaller as you go.

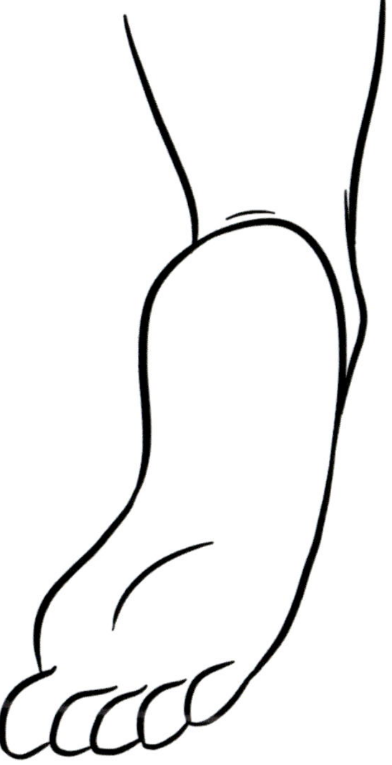

5.
Finalize your drawing with a dark pen.

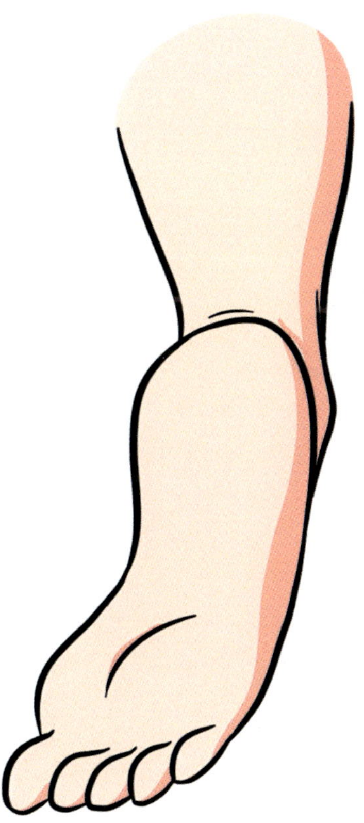

This is a good pose for when a character is kneeling down, or leaping in the air in joy! She could also be swimming away from the viewer.

For more interesting foot poses, get the male edition of this book. This could help you learn more about the structure and positions of feet.

BY MEI YU

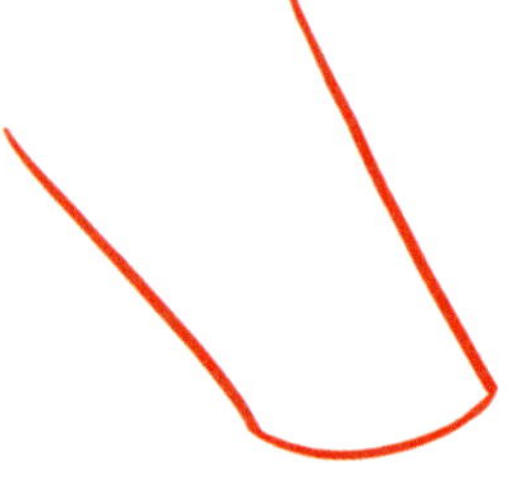

1.
Draw part of the leg pointed down, with the ankle thinner than the top.

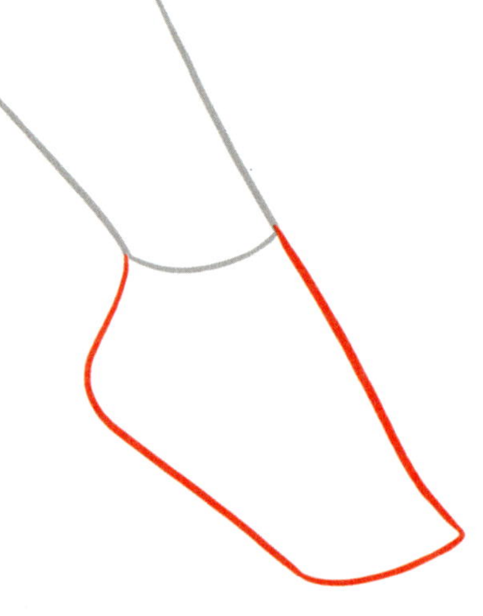

2.
Draw the foot like a curved rectangle, where the heel area is thicker than the toe area.

3.
Draw curved lines for the bone at the ankle, and the arch of the foot. Add a short rectangular shape to start the toes.

4.
Draw the big toe as a curve by the short rectangle, then divide the rectangle for the rest of the toes.

Pointed Foot

5.
Go over the final lines
with a dark pen or marker.

Try making the toe lines not too thick, so they can look more elegant.

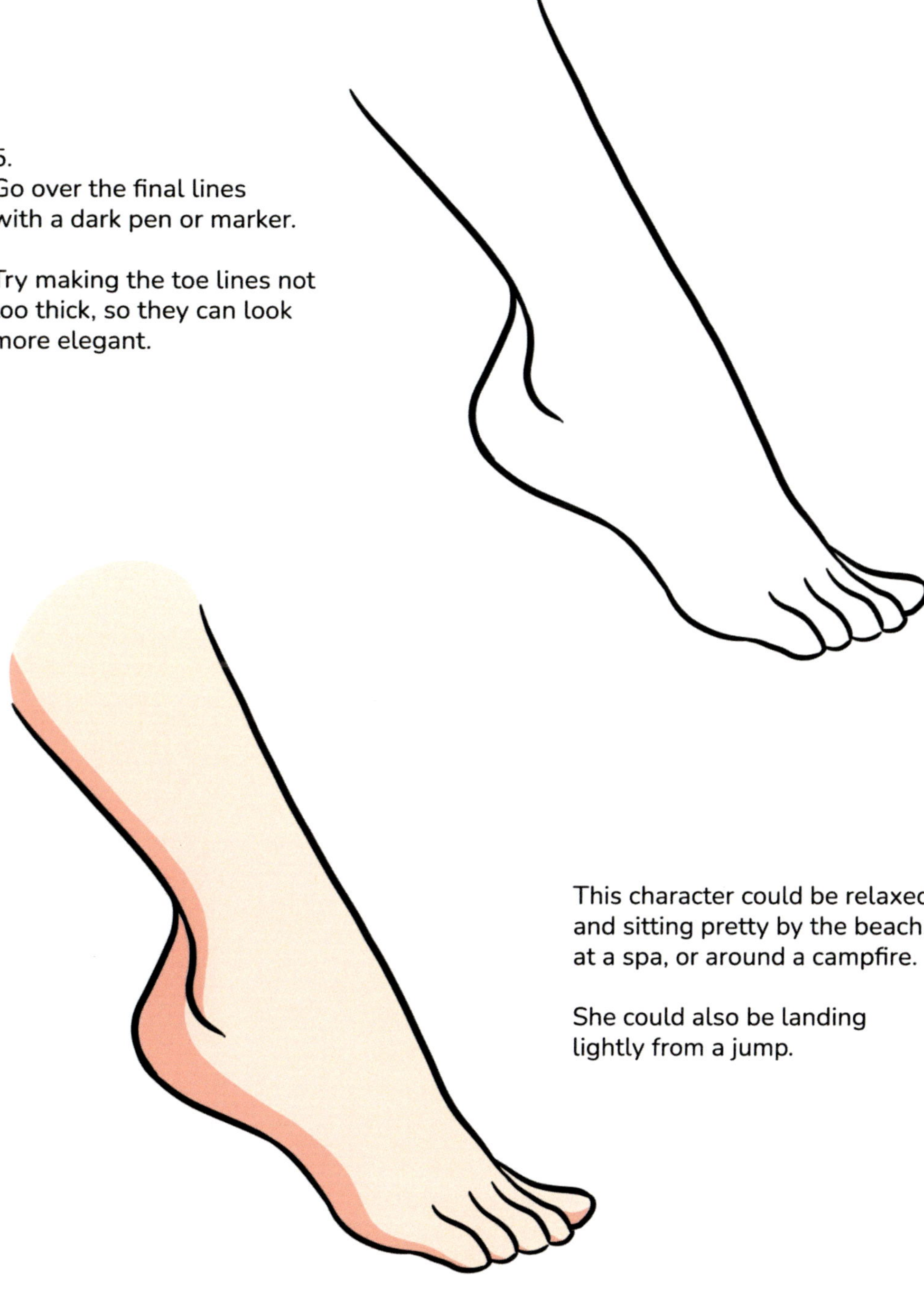

This character could be relaxed and sitting pretty by the beach, at a spa, or around a campfire.

She could also be landing lightly from a jump.

Lifted Gracefully

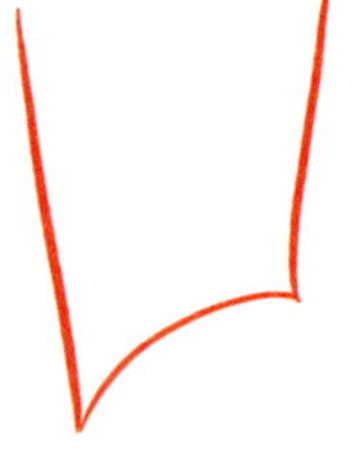

1.
Start with the ankle.

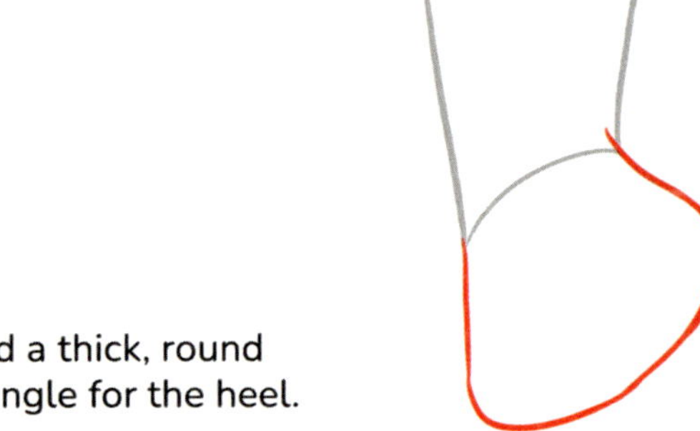

2.
Add a thick, round triangle for the heel.

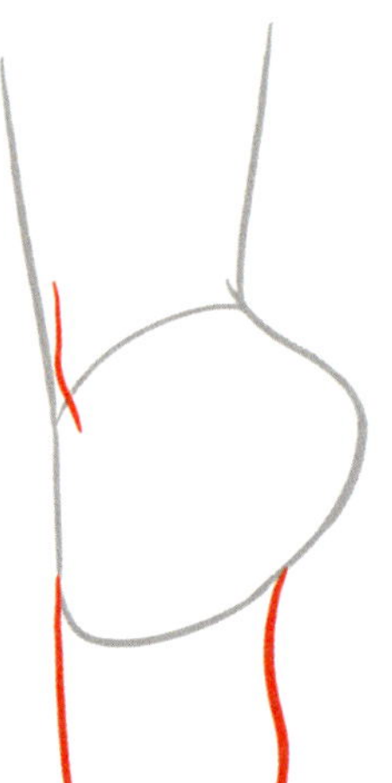

3.
Draw a curved rectangle to extend the basic foot shape.

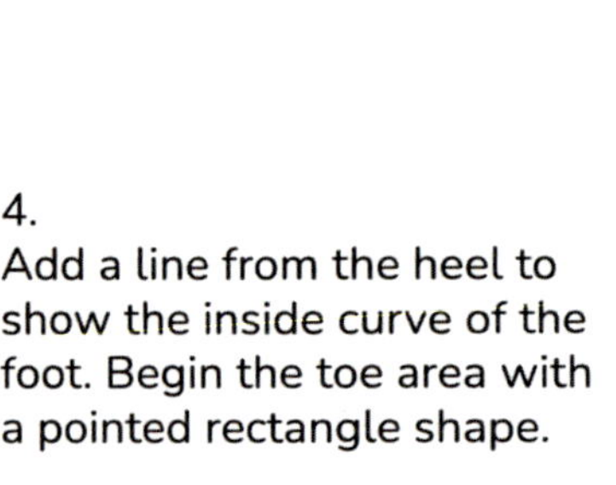

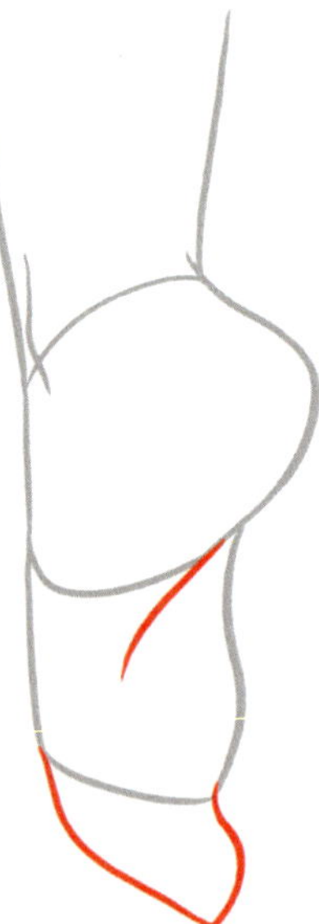

4.
Add a line from the heel to show the inside curve of the foot. Begin the toe area with a pointed rectangle shape.

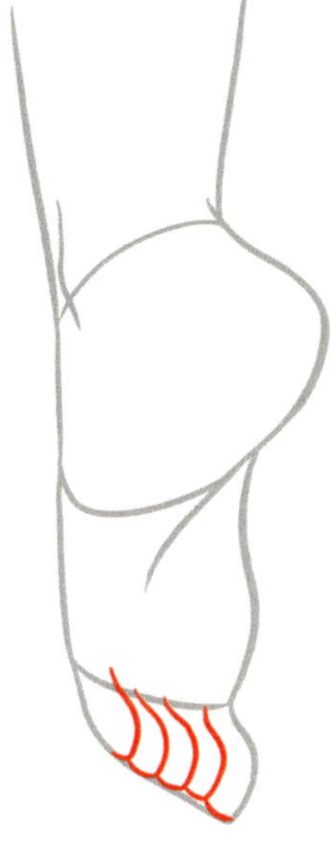

5.
Make the toes by dividing the pointed rectangle shape.

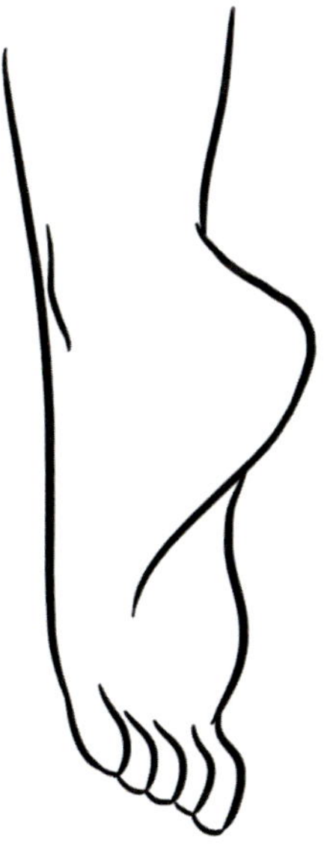

6.
Erase extra lines then use a dark pen or marker to go over the final drawing.

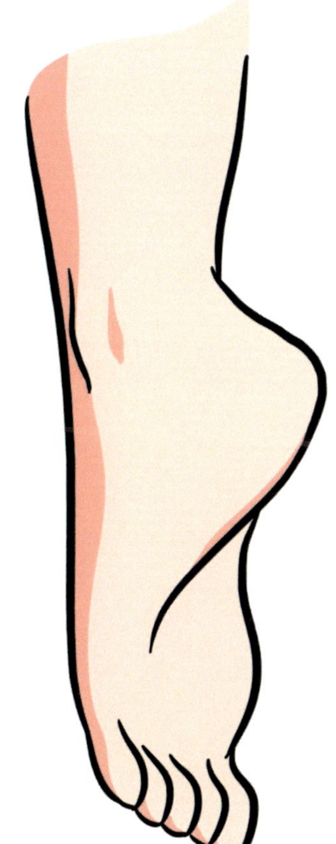

This is a nice graceful pose - the character could be an angel, flying or hovering in the air. She could also have just leapt up during a volleyball game, or at a trampoline competition.

Standing (From Behind)

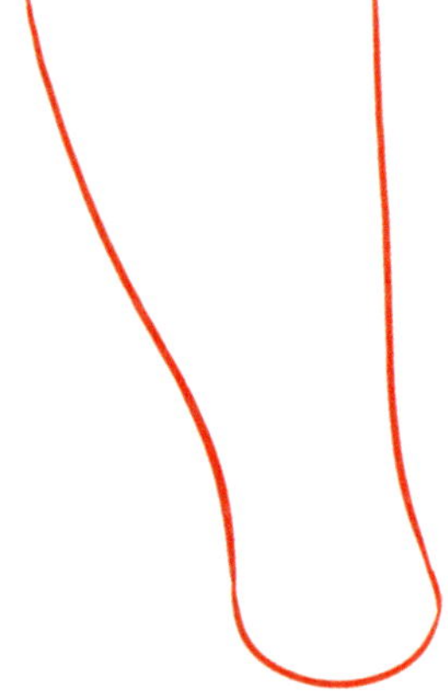

1.
Draw the lower leg coming down into the slim ankle.

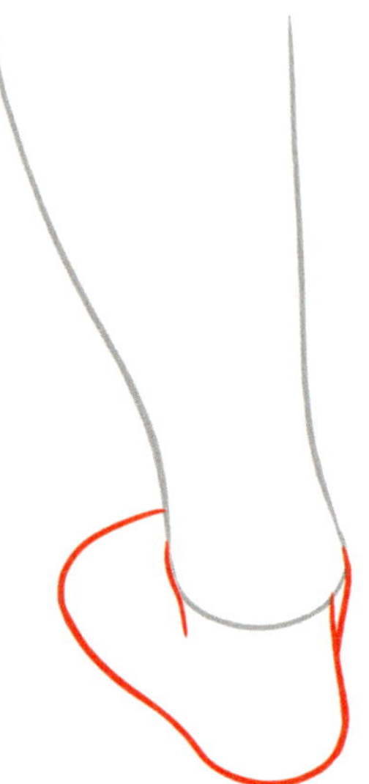

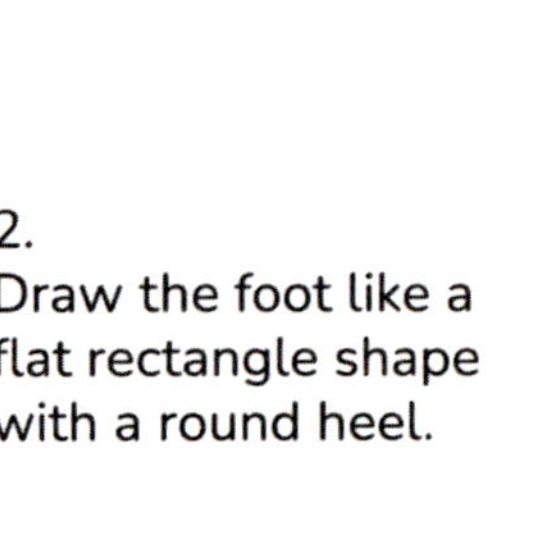

2.
Draw the foot like a flat rectangle shape with a round heel.

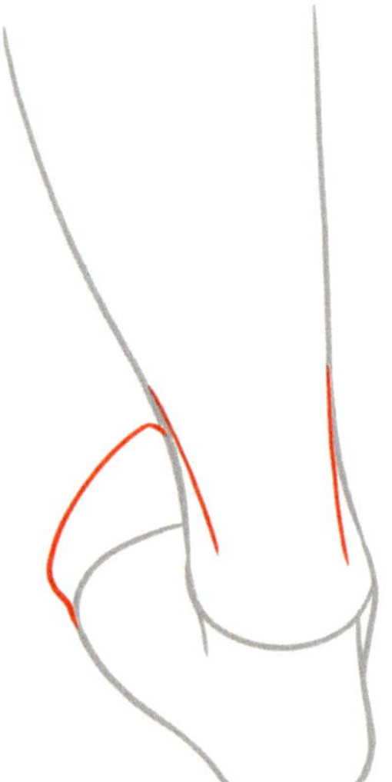

3.
Draw the toes as a large shape first.

Show the structure of the leg more with two lines coming down into the back side of the heel. Make these lines point towards each other slightly for a more organic look.

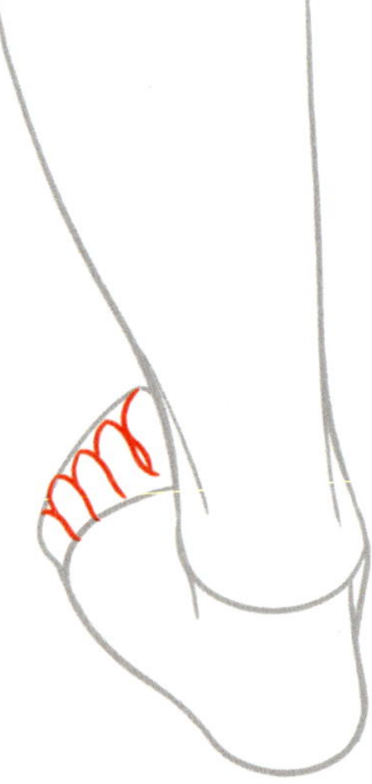

4.
Add curved toes in the shape. The big toe can be a bit hidden from view in this angle.

BY MEI YU

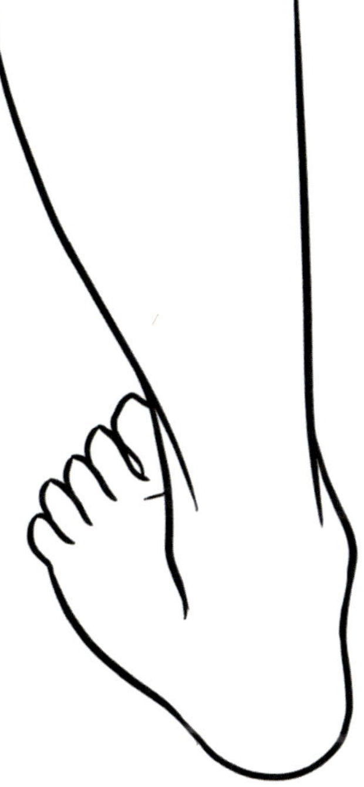

5.
Finalize your drawing after extra lines are erased.

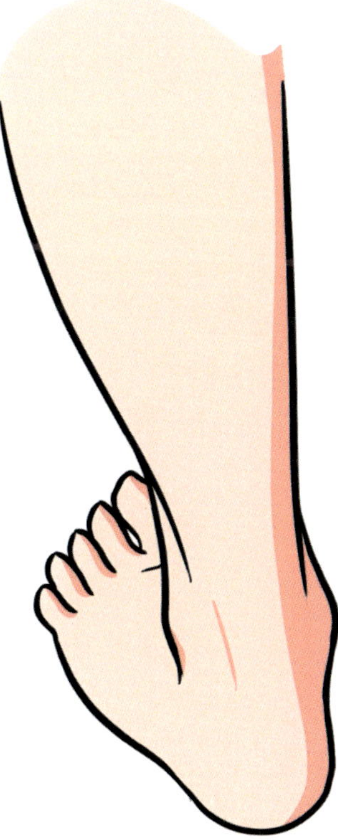

This is a handy pose for when a character is standing, and you want to show the back view of her.

Showing a character from behind can evoke different feelings depending on the situation, like sadness, longing, or mystery.

You could draw simple things in the scene to help with the atmosphere of the drawing, such as drawing gentle ocean waves by her foot, or a bathroom scale, or a flower garden.

Foot Facing Up at Angle

BY MEI YU

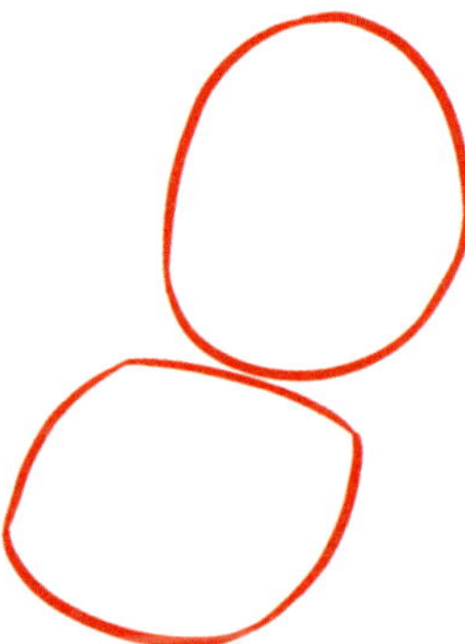

1.
Summarize the foot into two basic shapes first.

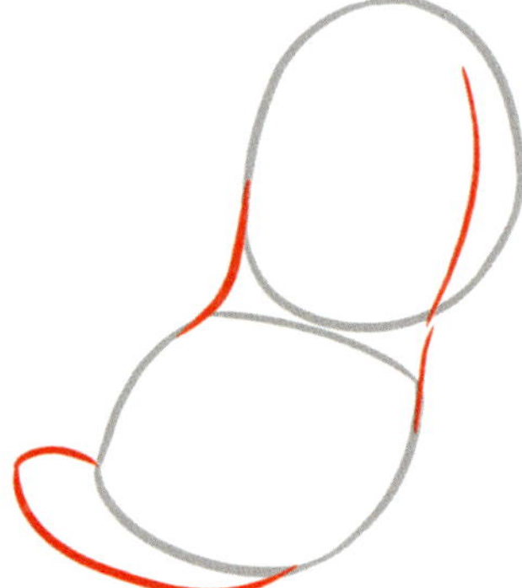

2.
Connect the two shapes together to form the sides of the foot. Then, draw a curve for the toes to start.

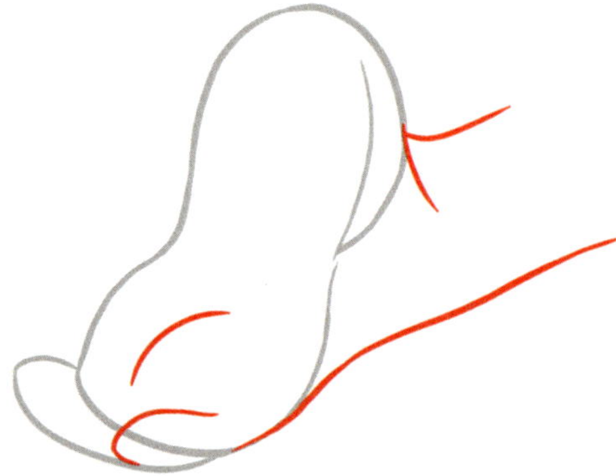

3.
Draw lines from the foot to form the ankle. Then, add curves for the surface of the foot, and the big toe.

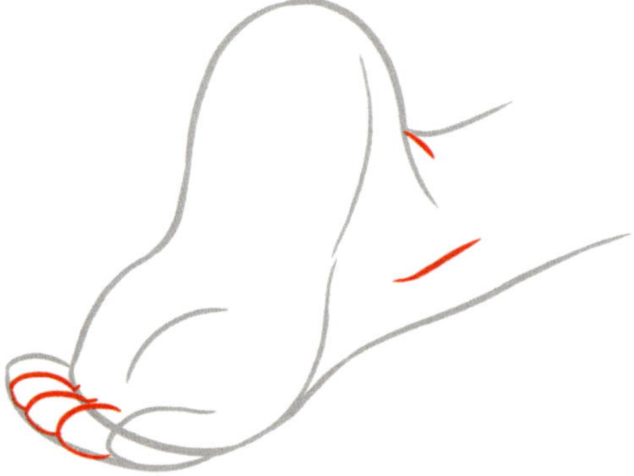

4.
Draw the other toes as curved lines, and add finishing touches to show the structure of the foot better.

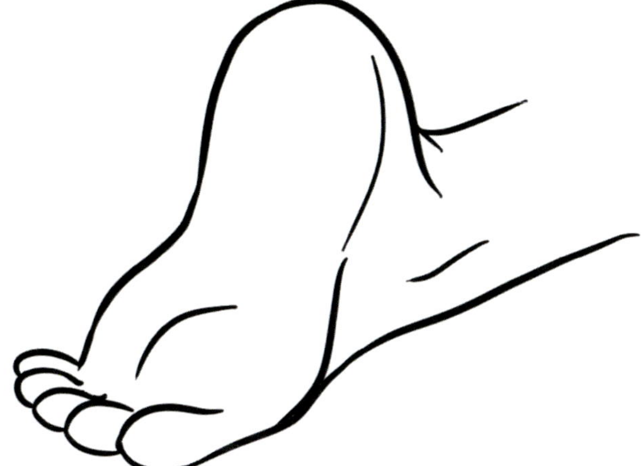

5.
Erase extra lines before finalizing your drawing.

This pose can be great for when your character is lying in bed, chilling with her phone, or sunbathing at the beach.

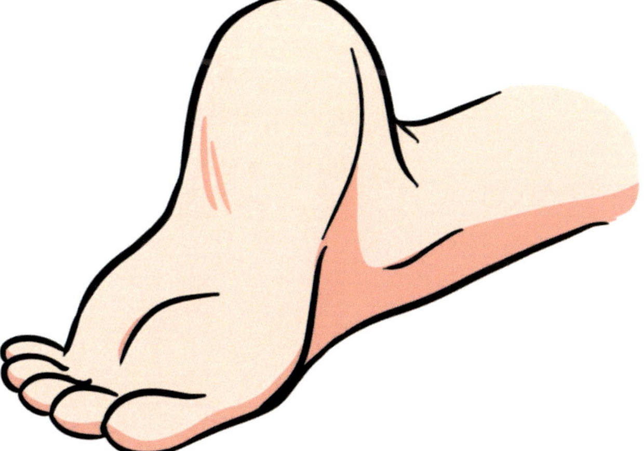

Feet can be very expressive, as well as hands. To practice different hand poses for male and female characters, check out my other books ***Draw 1 Hand in 20 Poses*** (Male and Female editions).

Up on Toes (Side View)

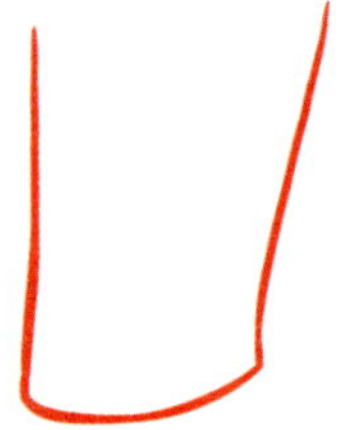

1.
Start with the ankle.

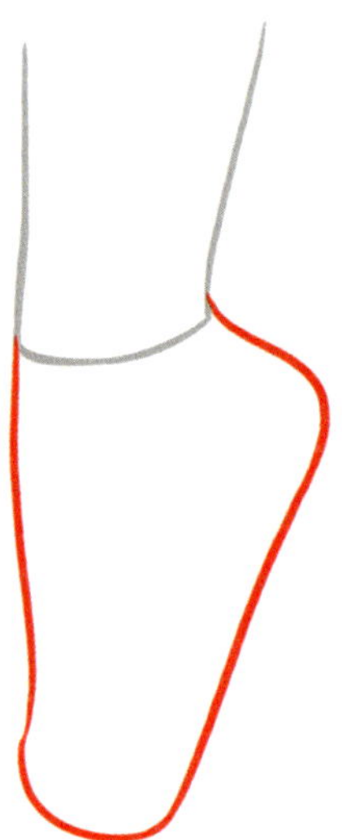

2.
Angle the foot down.
The basic shape is like a rounded rectangle with a large corner for the heel.

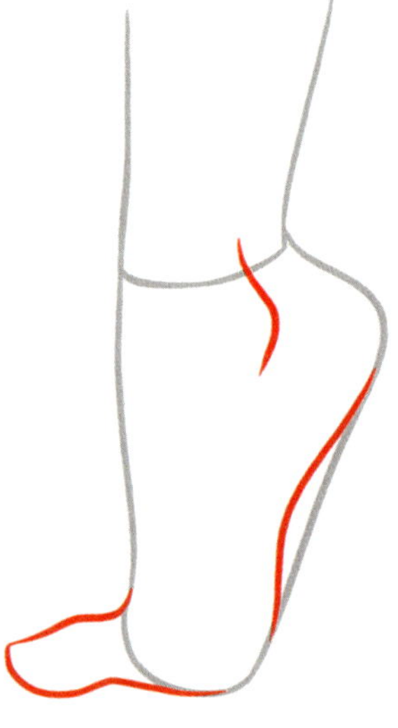

3.
Draw a curve to show the arch in the foot.

Add the ankle bone line, then the big toe.

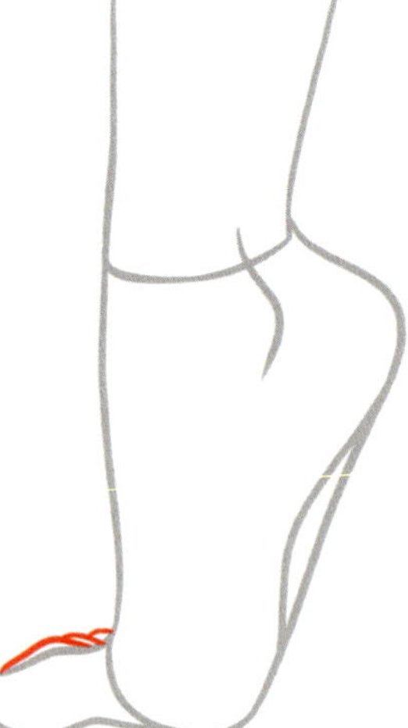

4.
Add the other toes poking out from behind.

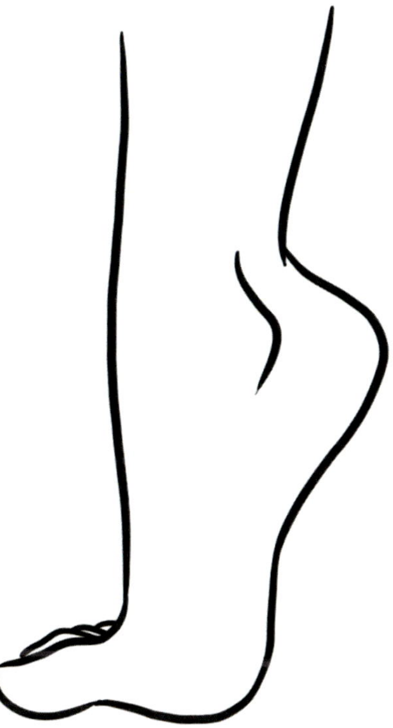

5.
Finalize your drawing with your choice of a black pen or outliner.

Try this pose for characters who need to reach something high up, showing off their height, or doing an elegant dance routine.

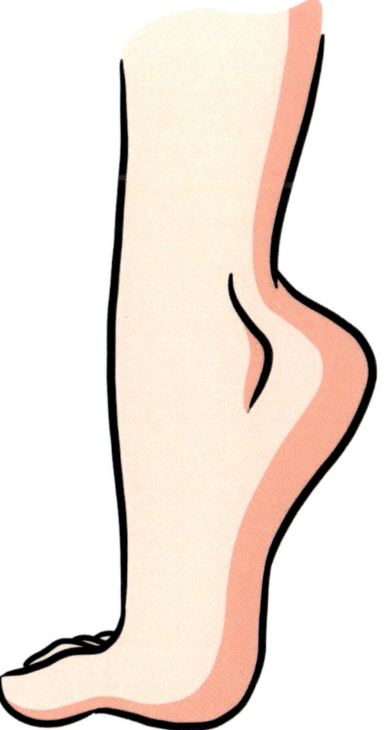

Stepped on Something

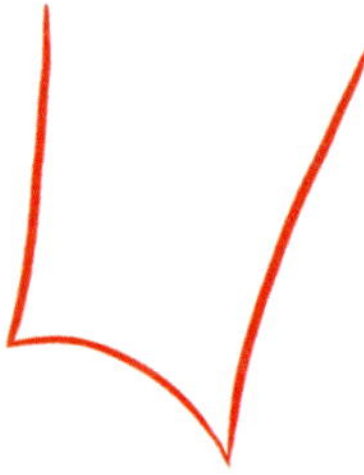

1.
Begin with the ankle area.

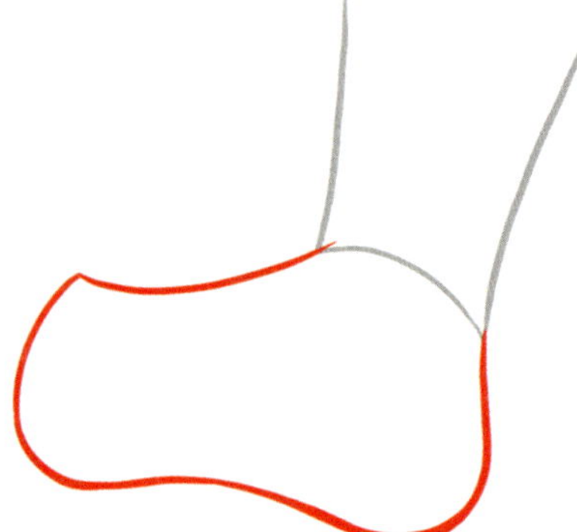

2.
Draw the foot like a rounded rectangle, with a large heel.

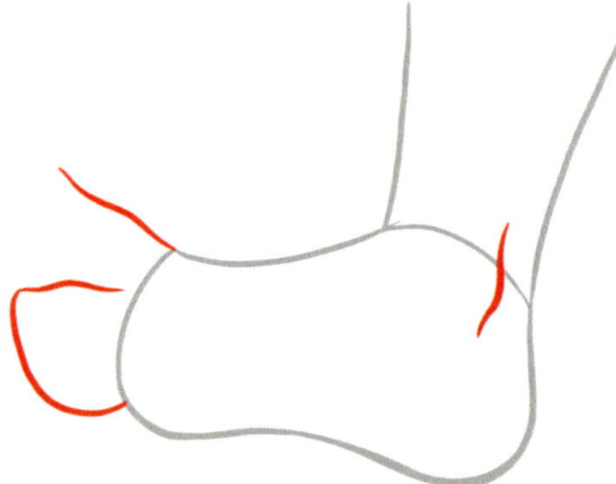

3.
Begin the toes with a line for the big toe, then a small area for the other toes.

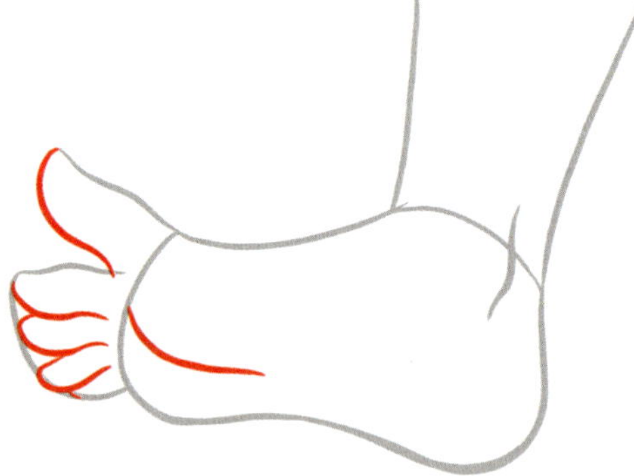

4.
A good way to show a painful pose is to separate the toes. The gap between the big toe and the rest of the toes can hint at surprise or discomfort.

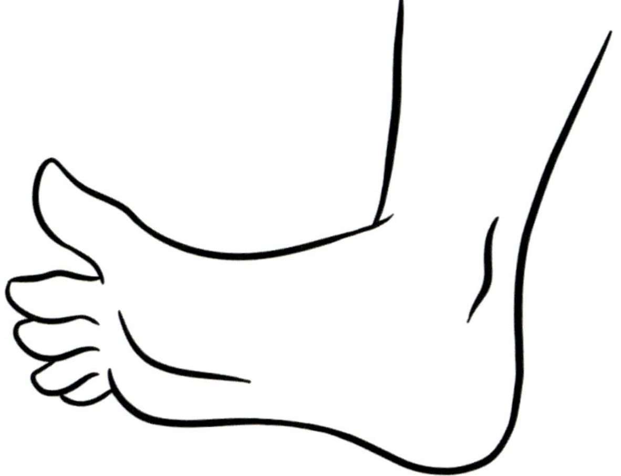

5.
Draw over the final lines with a dark pen, marker, or outliner.

This pose is great when you want to show a character in surprise, disgust, or pain after she stepped on something.

She could also be jumping in the air, or about to land on something.

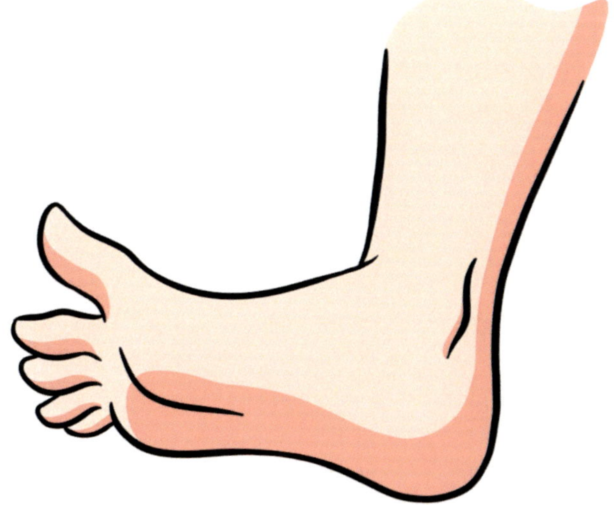

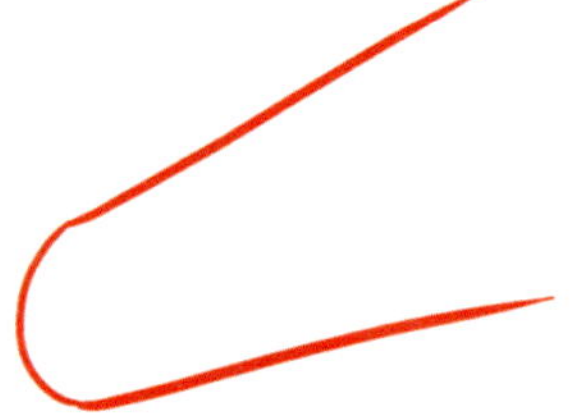

1.
Start with the lower leg that tapers into the ankle.

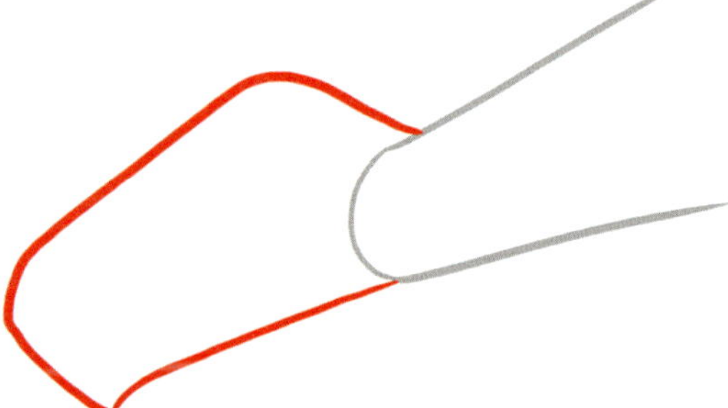

2.
Begin the foot as a basic shape first: a rounded triangle with a large corner for the heel.

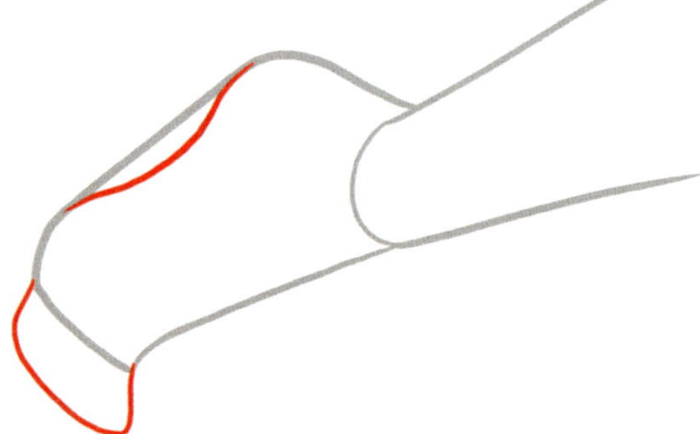

3.
Draw the curved arch, then the toe area.

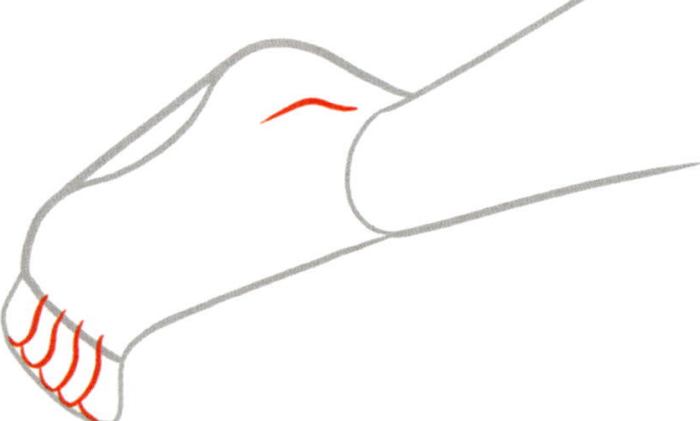

4.
Divide the toe area into individual toes. Try using slightly curved lines so the toes will look more natural.

5.
Once you're done, finalize your drawing with a dark pen or marker. Try to make the lines thin in the toes, so those details can be preserved.

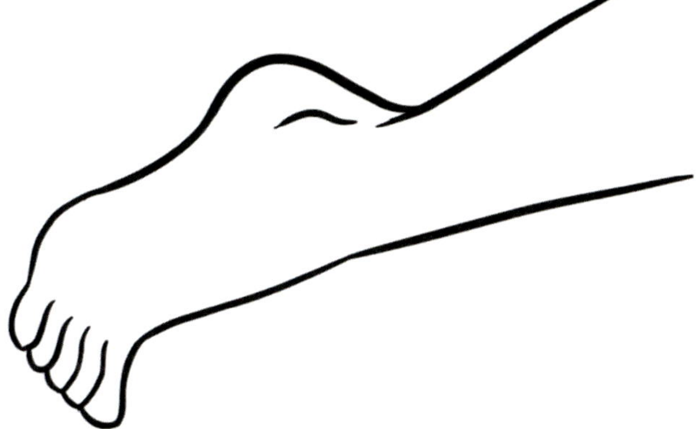

This character could be pushing off from a surface, leaping, or lying down.

She could be pushing off the wall of a swimming pool to do another lap, or a superhero jumping from a falling building.

Try tilting the foot in different angles to suit your character's situation. Keep up the good work!

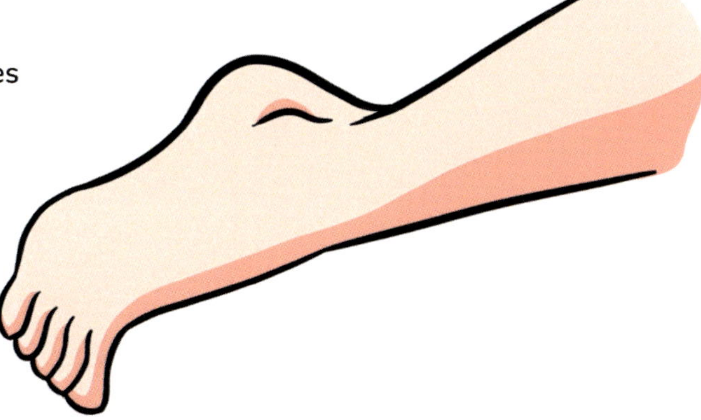

Stepping Lightly

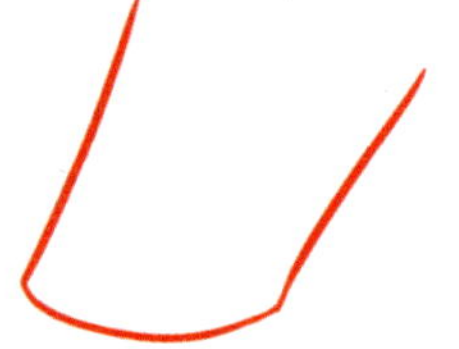

1.
Draw the ankle tilted down.

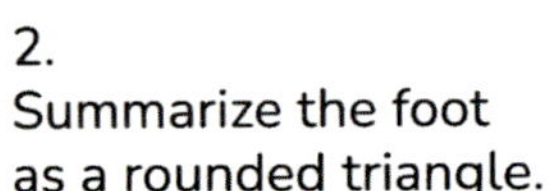

2.
Summarize the foot as a rounded triangle.

Try to make the toe area in the front smaller and more narrow than the heel.

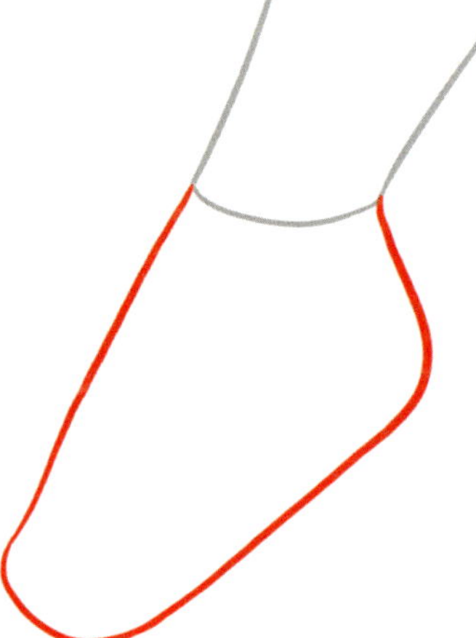

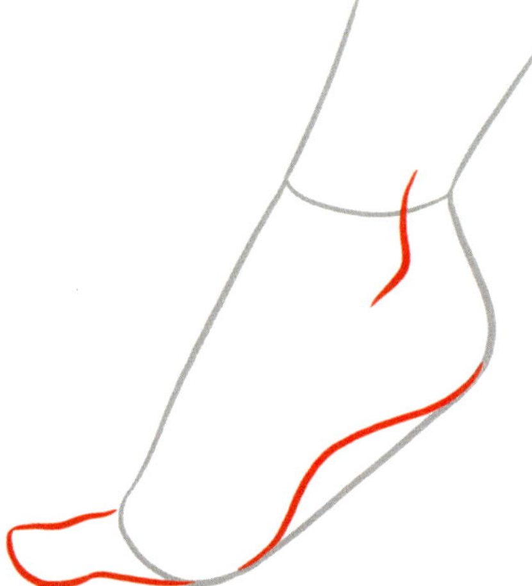

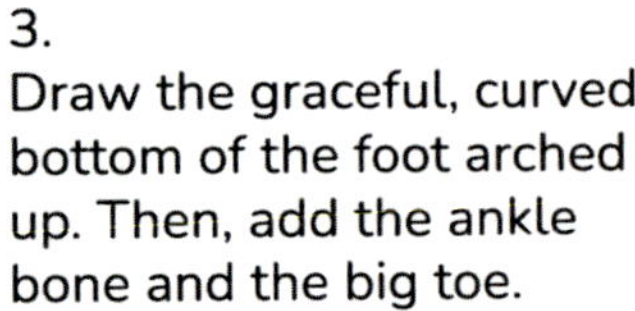

3.
Draw the graceful, curved bottom of the foot arched up. Then, add the ankle bone and the big toe.

Use soft lines so the foot looks more natural. Keep your wrists loose when drawing.

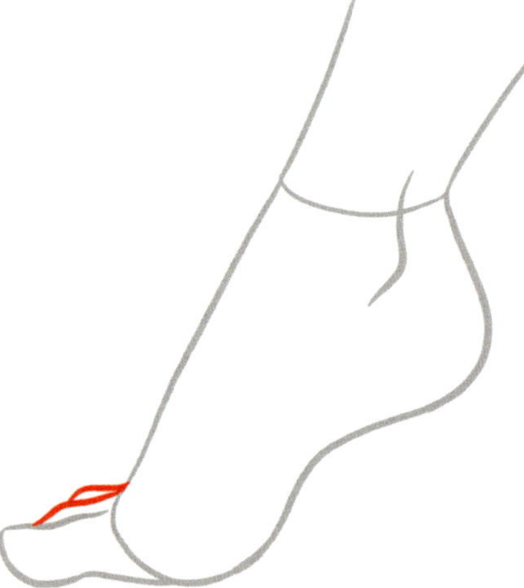

4.
Now add a few more toes to show a little of the other side.

This is also a great way to add more dimension to your drawing.

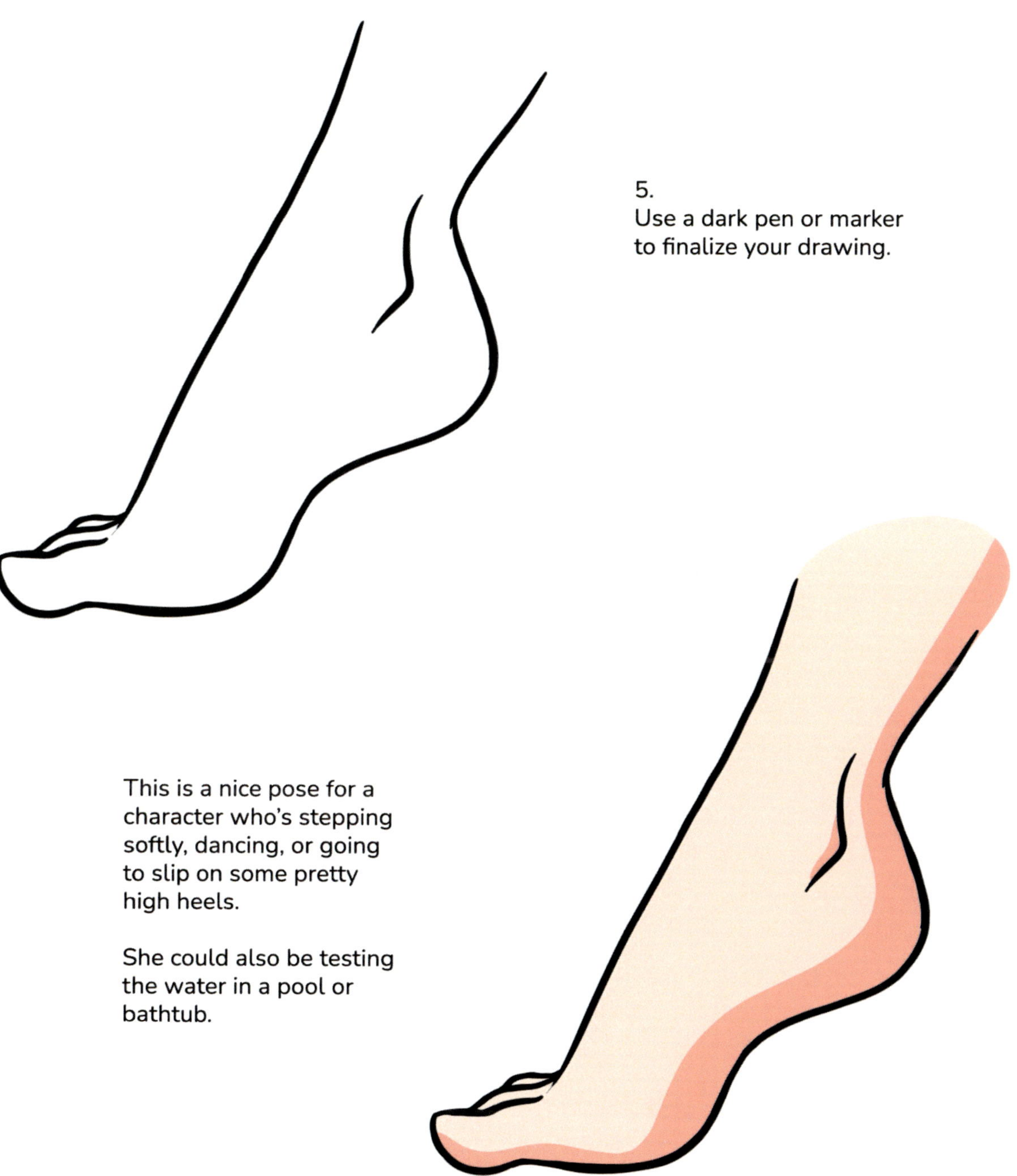

5.
Use a dark pen or marker to finalize your drawing.

This is a nice pose for a character who's stepping softly, dancing, or going to slip on some pretty high heels.

She could also be testing the water in a pool or bathtub.

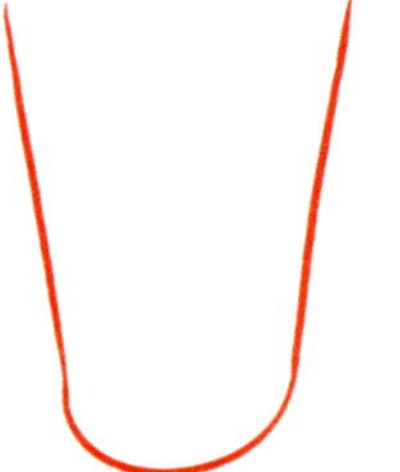

1.
Draw the ankle down. Keep the joint area smaller than the upper area.

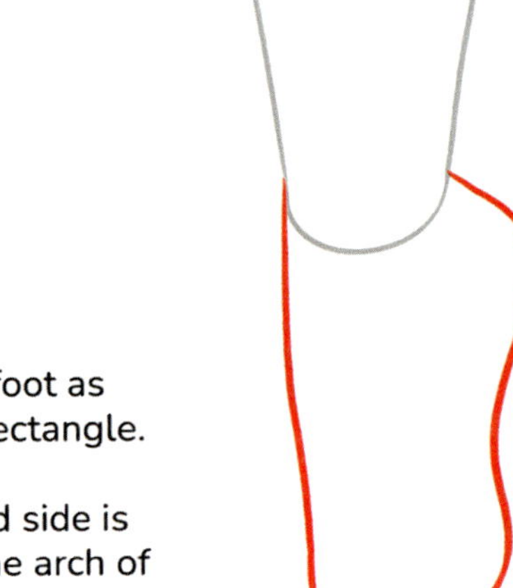

2.
Draw the foot as a curved rectangle.

The curved side is to show the arch of the foot.

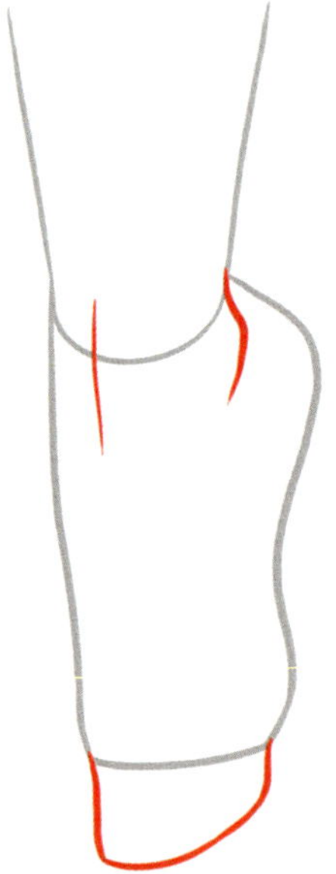

3.
Add a small line on top of the foot to show that area is stretched.

Draw the ankle bone and the toe area.

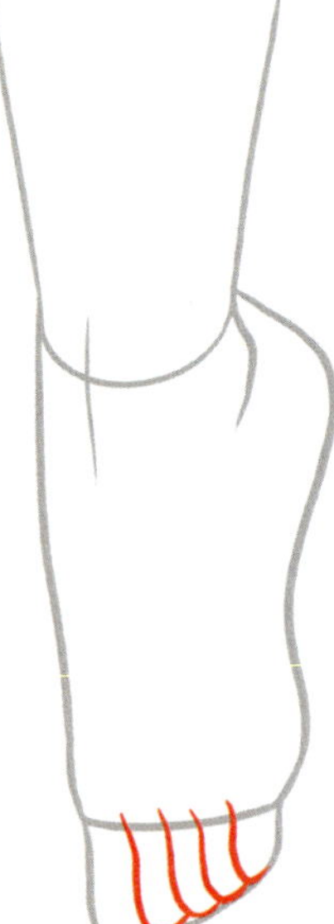

4.
Draw the toes using curved lines with round tips.

Dipping Toes

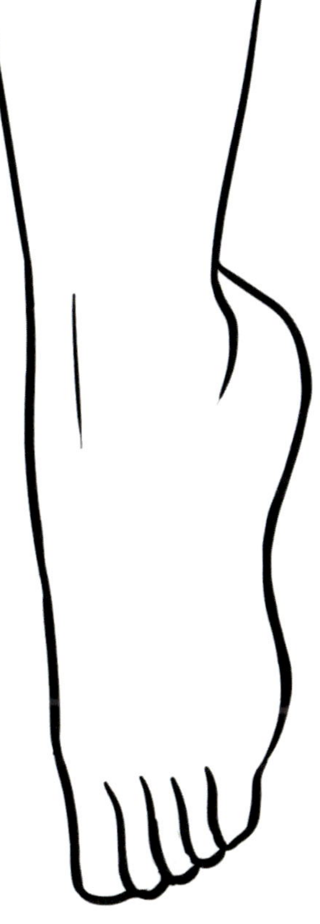

5.
Erase extra lines, then finalize your drawing with your choice of a dark pen, black outliner, or brush pen.

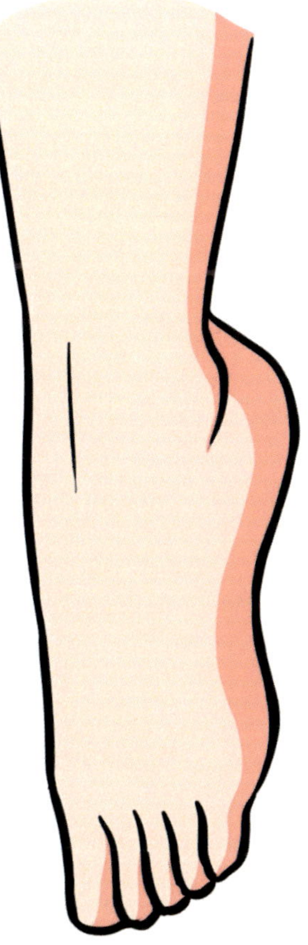

This character could be dipping her toes in the pool or hot spring.

She could also be leaping from a diving board, or tiptoeing to sneak up on a friend.

Relaxed

BY MEI YU

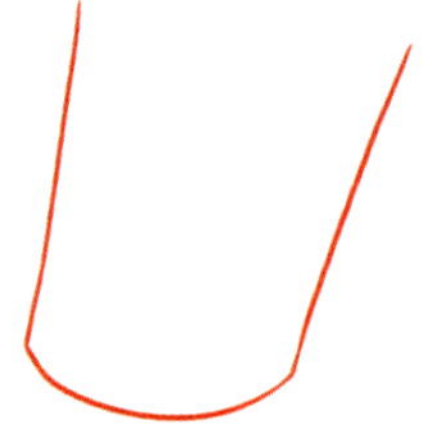

1.
Draw the ankle.

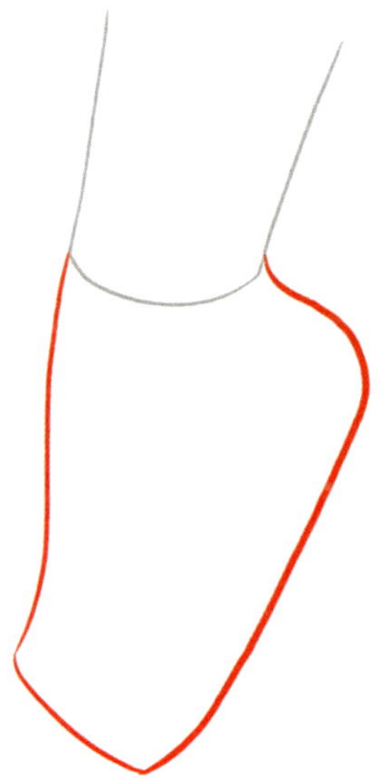

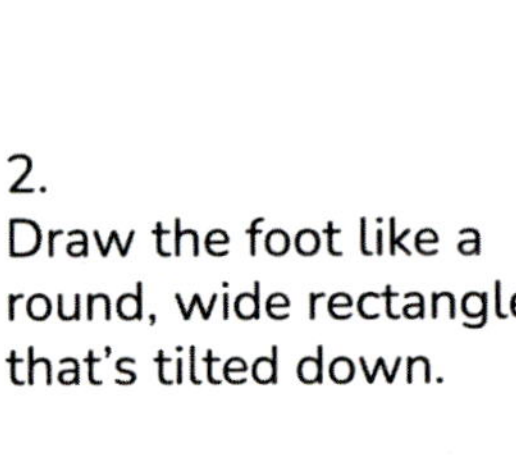

2.
Draw the foot like a round, wide rectangle that's tilted down.

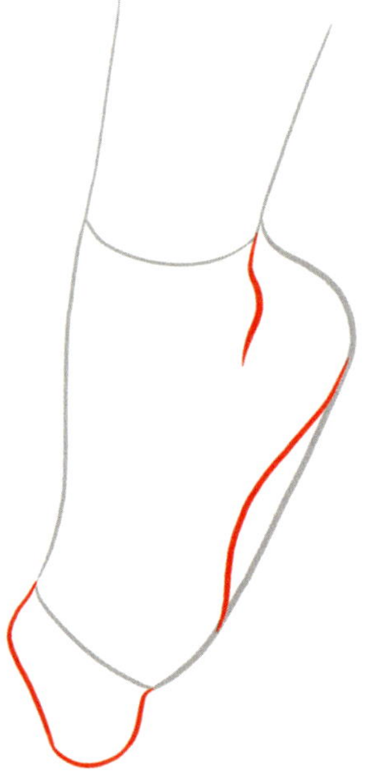

3.
Add a curve inside the bottom part of the foot to show the arch. Add the toe area.

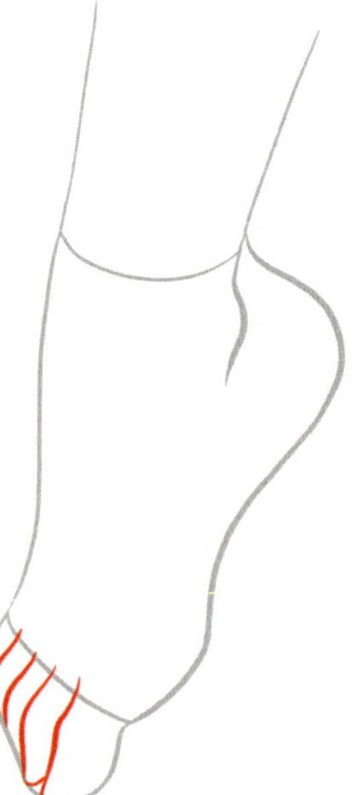

4.
A simple way to draw toes is to divide the toe area using curved lines.

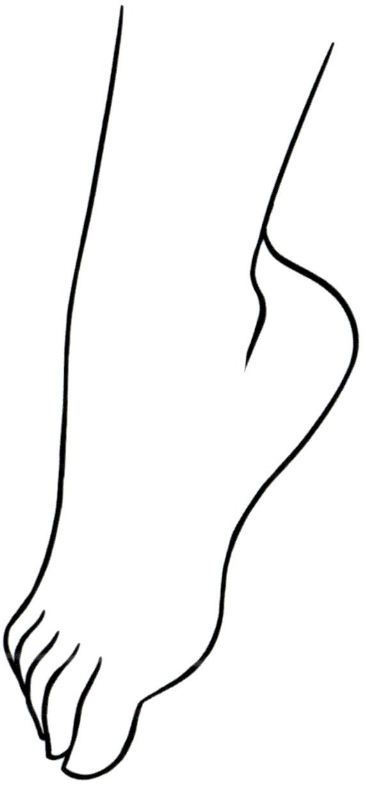

5.
After drawing, use a dark pen to go over the final lines.

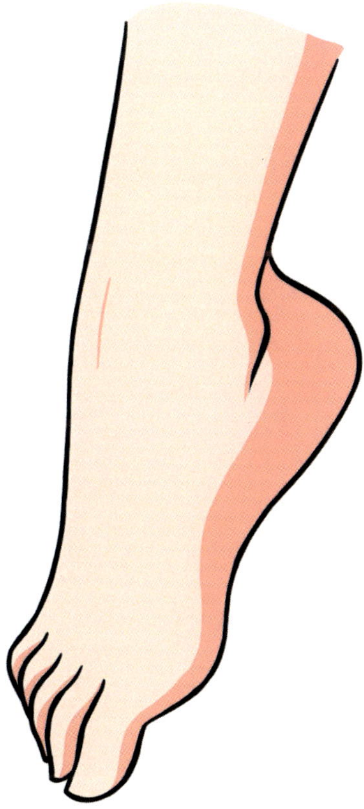

This is a nice pose for a character who is relaxed. She could be hanging her feet over an edge, or stepping softly.

Try drawing similar poses with the male edition of this book so you can understand how to draw different feet for your characters!

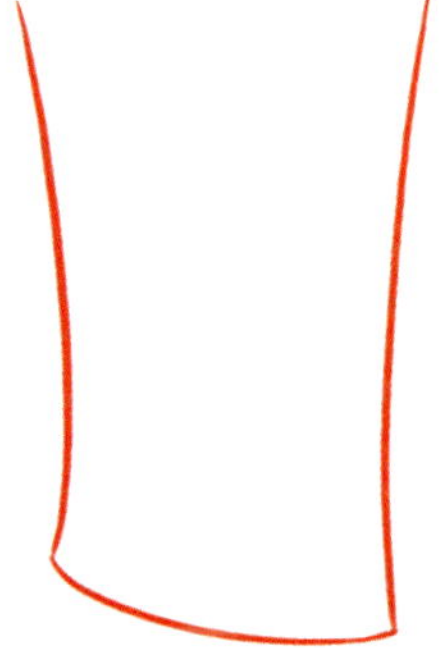

1.
Draw the lower leg tapering into the slim ankle.

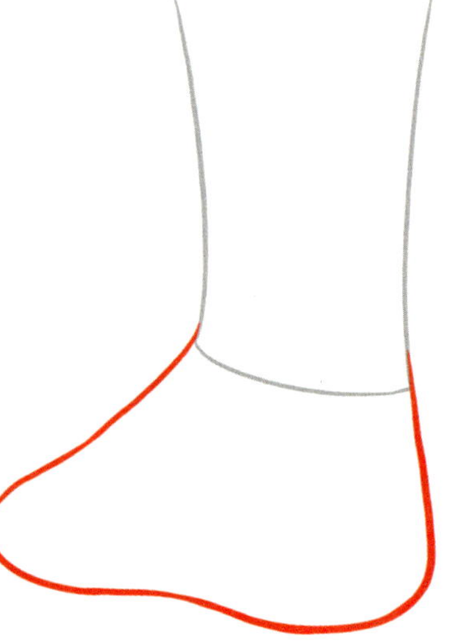

2.
Begin the foot as a soft, round triangle. Make sure the heel area is wide and curved.

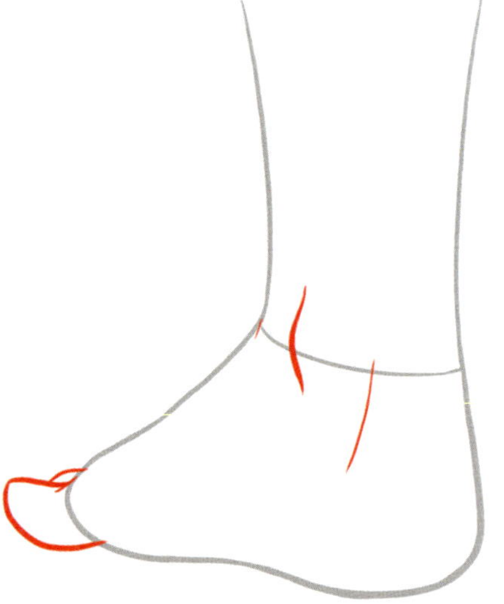

3.
Draw the big toe and a little bit of the next toe. Add some lines in the foot to show the structure better.

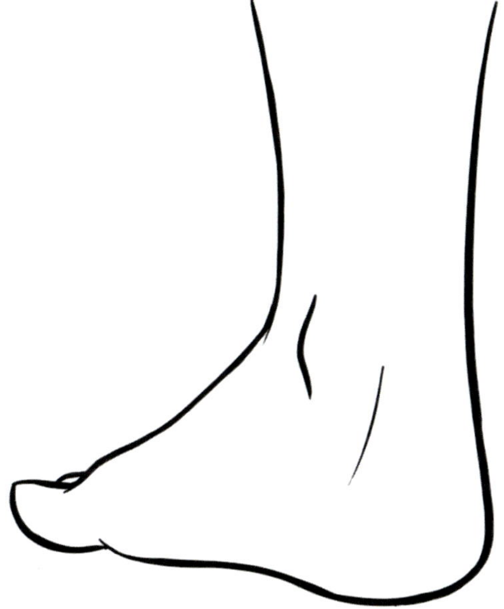

4.
Finalize the drawing after erasing extra lines.

Great job!

This is a good pose to show a character standing in front of the viewer.

Keep practicing from my other books in the ***Draw 1 in 20*** series! Then you can design professional-looking characters from head to toe!

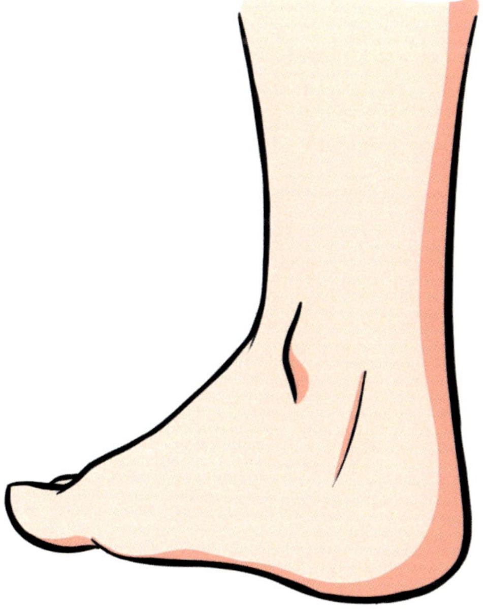

Foot in the Air

BY MEI YU

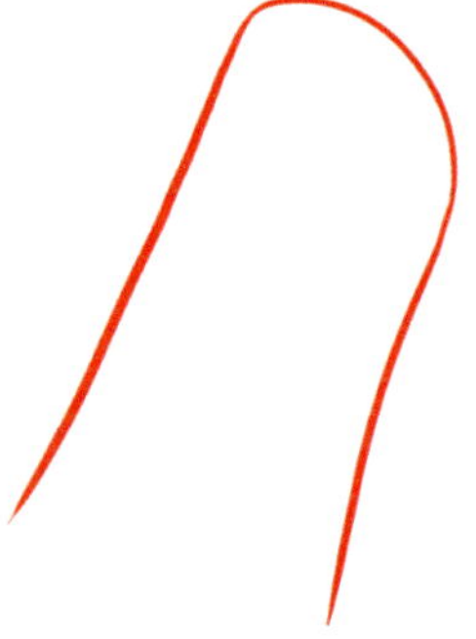

1.
Start with the lower leg tilting up.

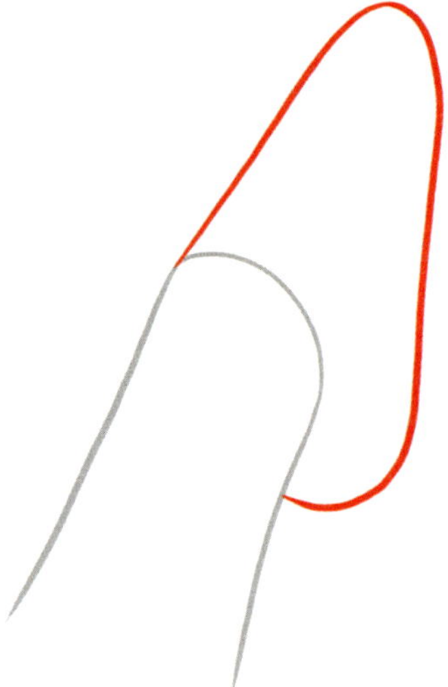

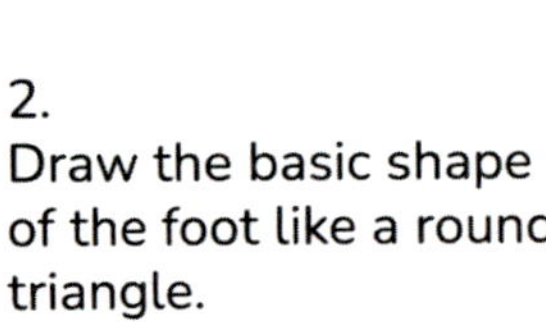

2.
Draw the basic shape of the foot like a round triangle.

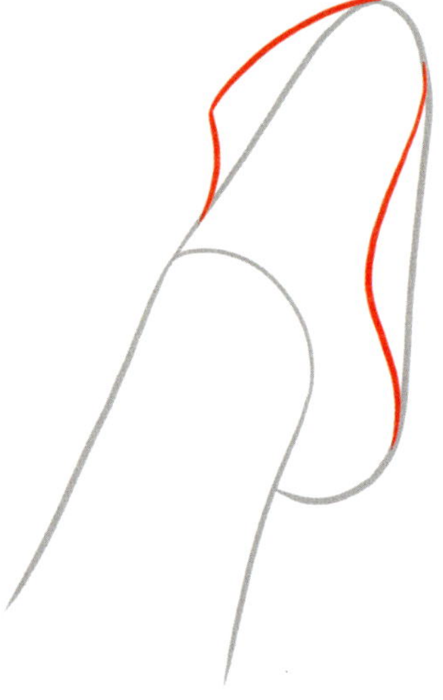

3.
Add a curved line in the arch of the foot on the bottom, then draw more of the foot on top.

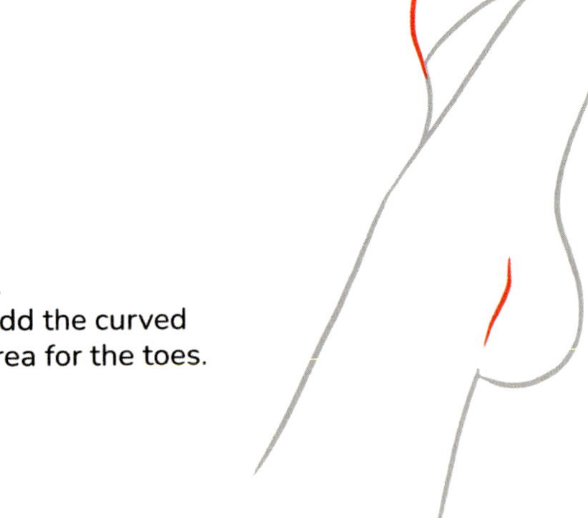

4.
Add the curved area for the toes.

BY MEI YU

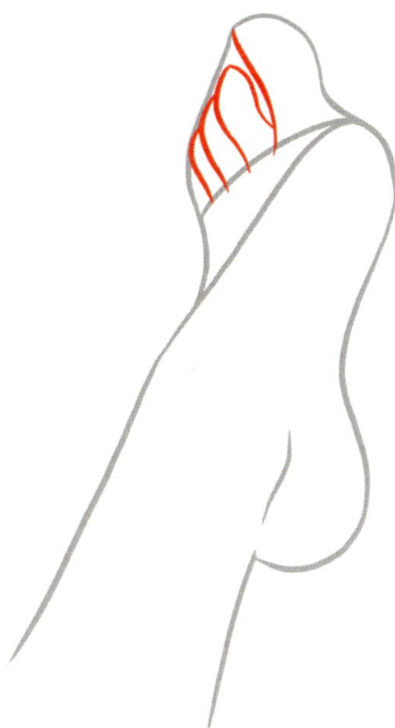

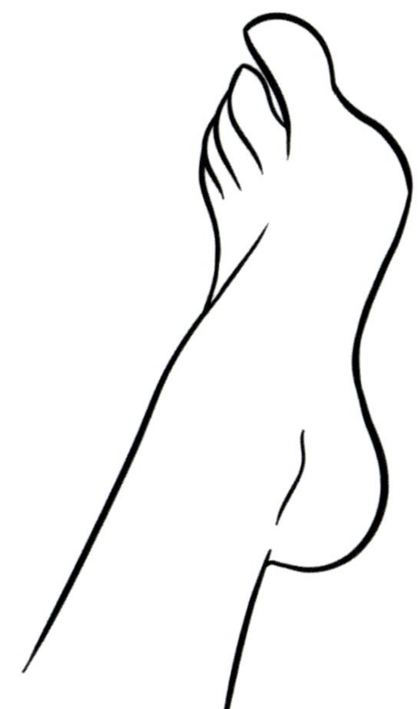

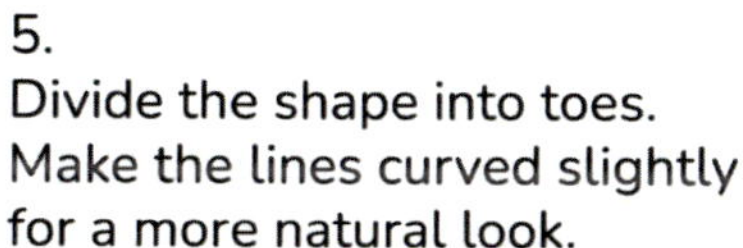

5.
Divide the shape into toes. Make the lines curved slightly for a more natural look.

6.
Go over the final lines with a dark pen.

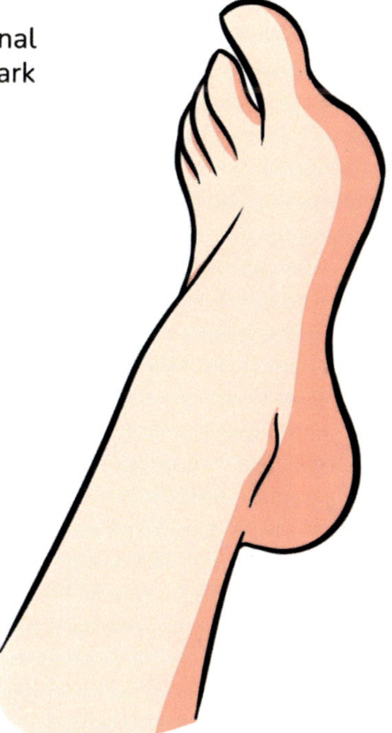

This pose can be good for when a character puts her foot up in the air to relax. Or, angle the foot down to make it look like she's stepping down on something.

Paperbacks

Mei Yu's Book Store

Over 80 books!

Coloring Books

New Releases

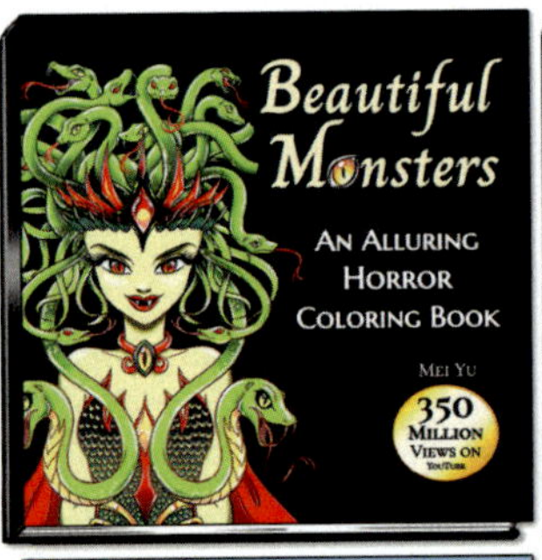

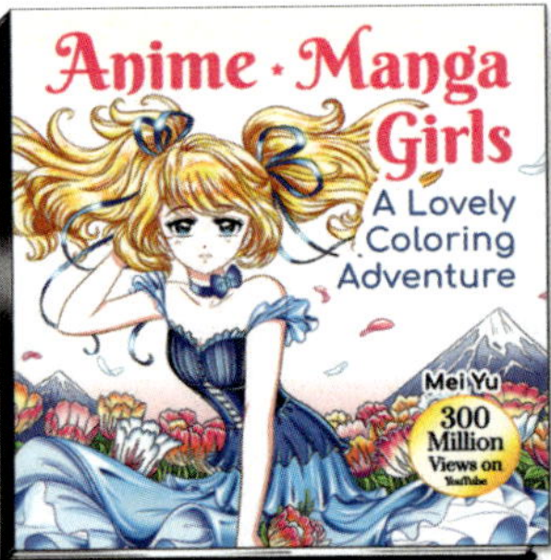

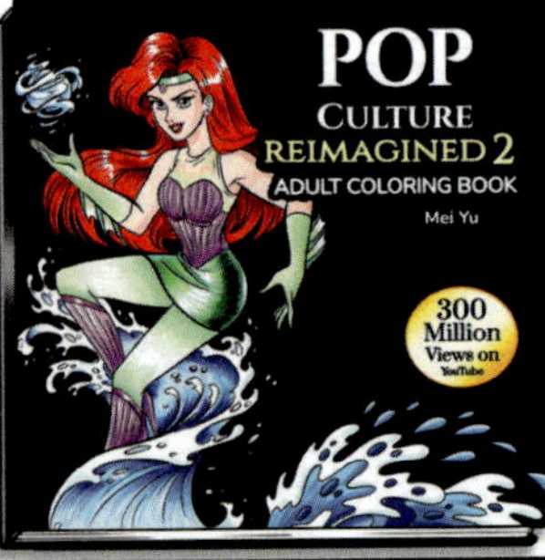

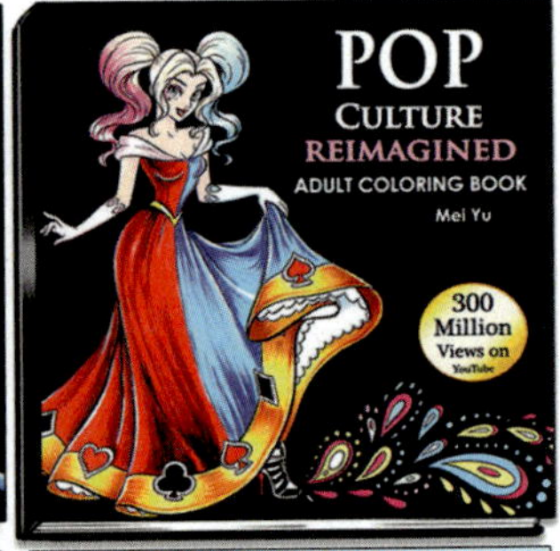

©Mei Yu Art Inc.

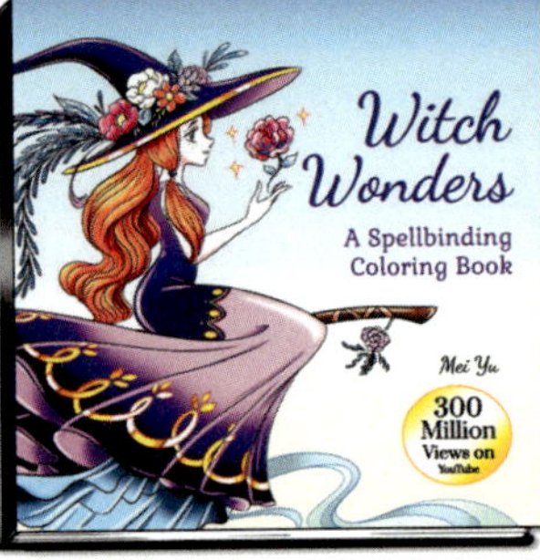

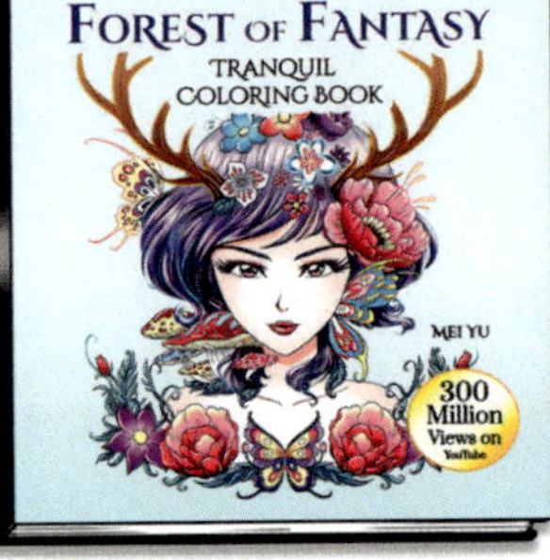

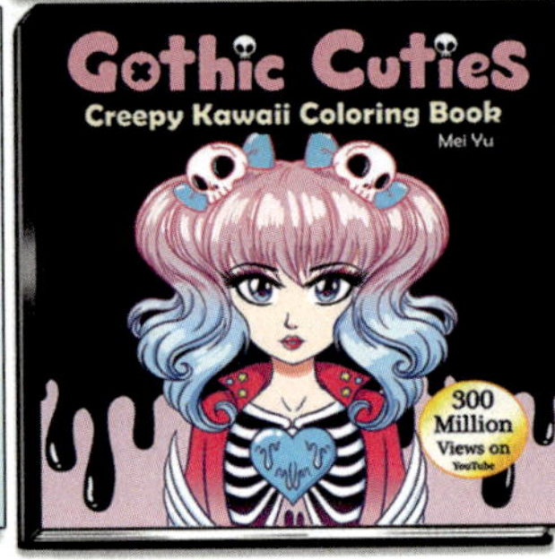

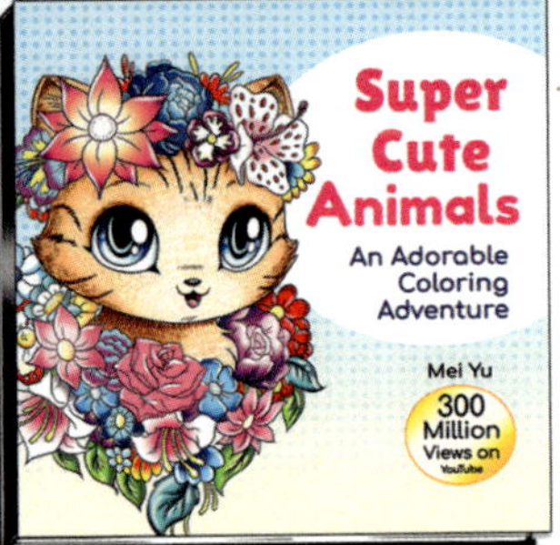

AND MORE...

Other sizes + hardcovers also available

How to Draw Books

New Release

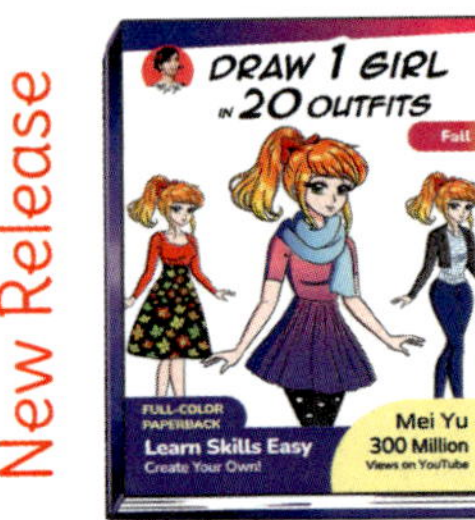

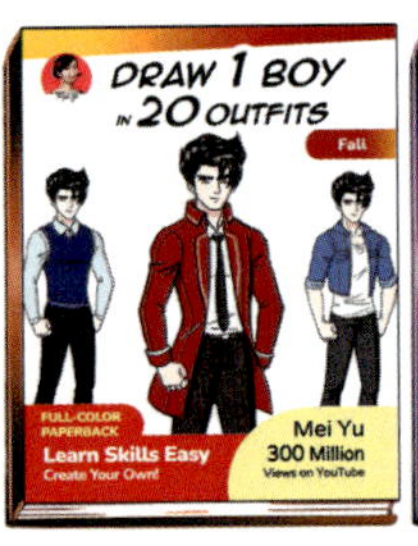

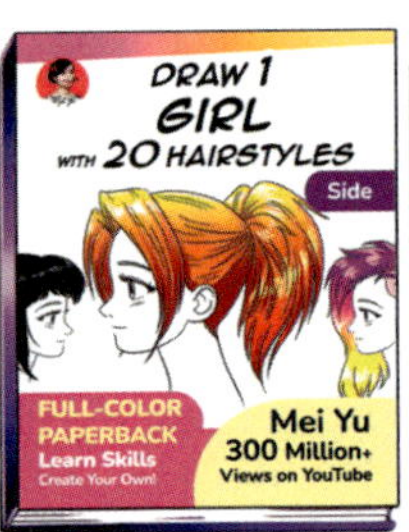

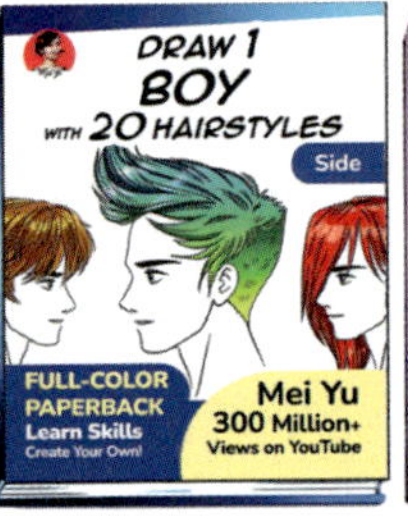

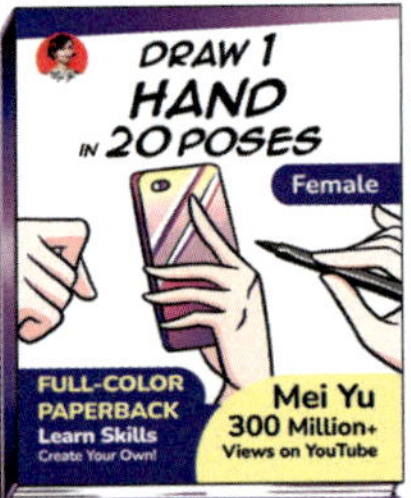

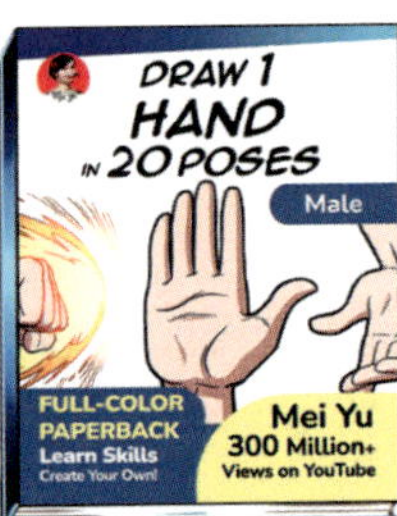

WorkBooks

New Release

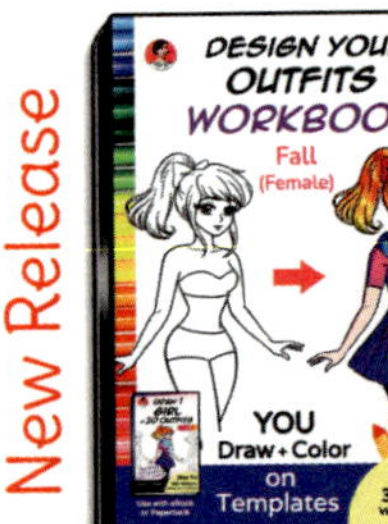

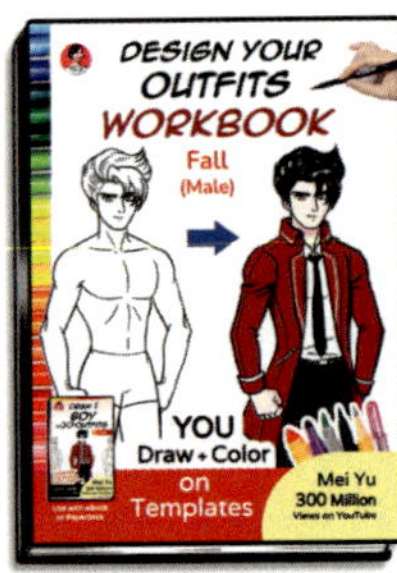

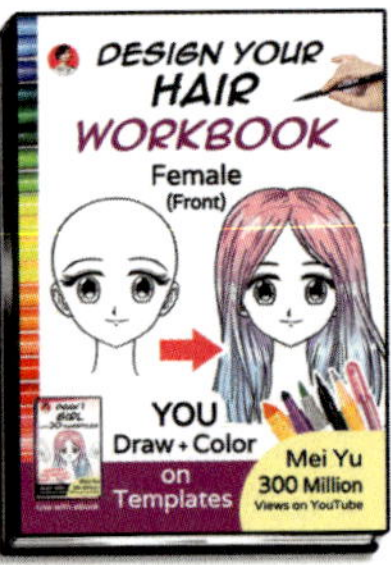

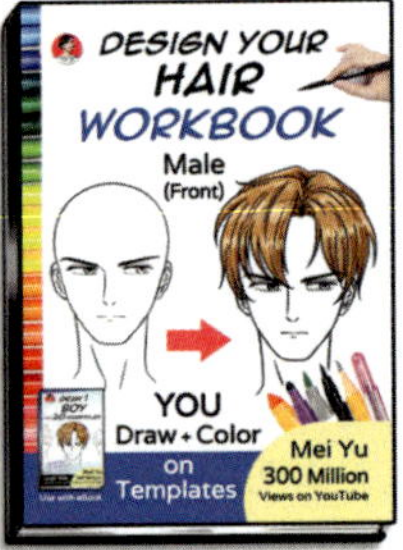

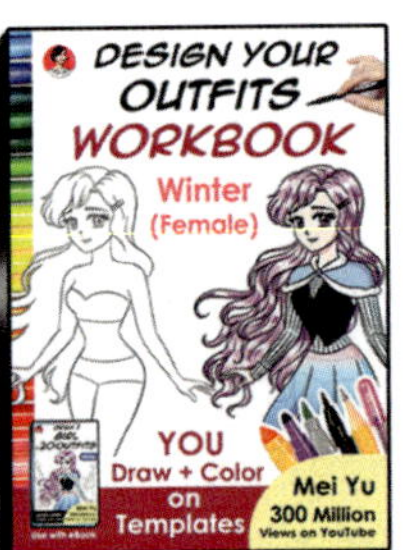

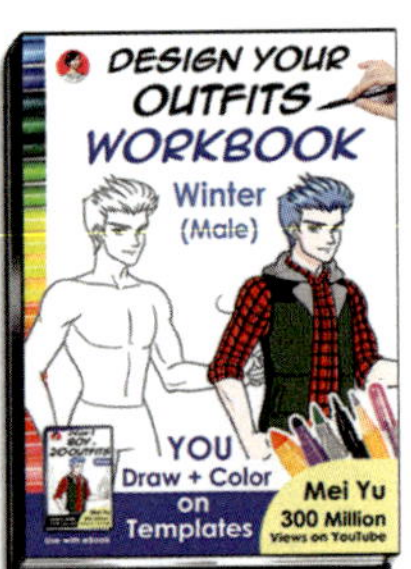

AND MORE...

Unleash Your Creativity  Own Now or Gift!

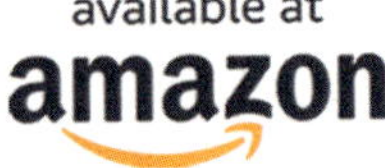

www.amazon.com/shop/meiyu

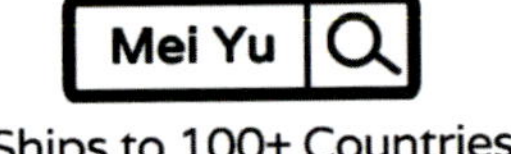

Ships to 100+ Countries

★ DRAW 1 IN 20 SERIES

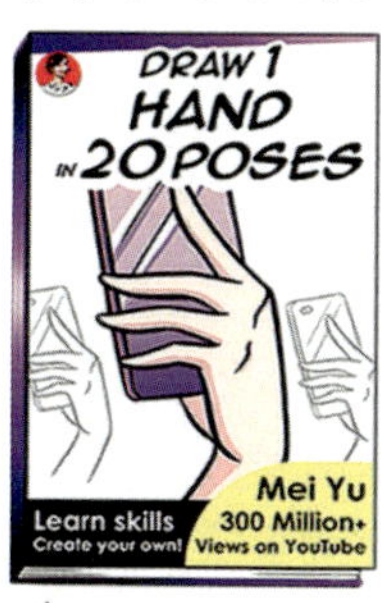

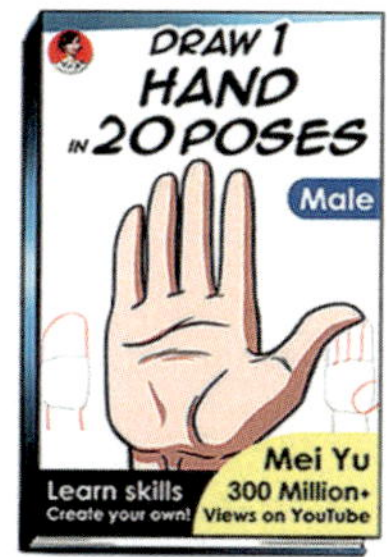

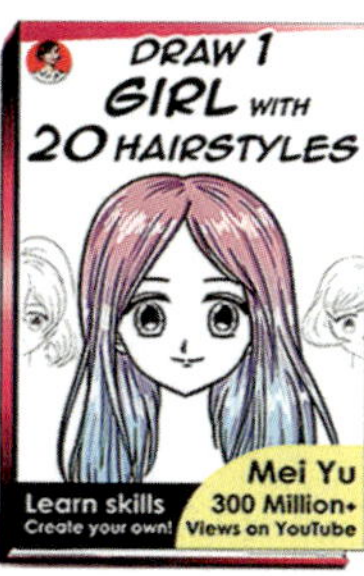

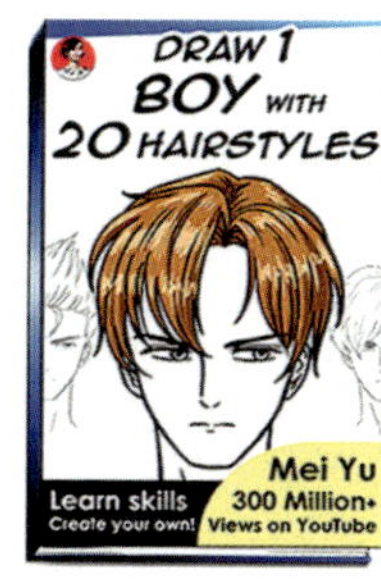

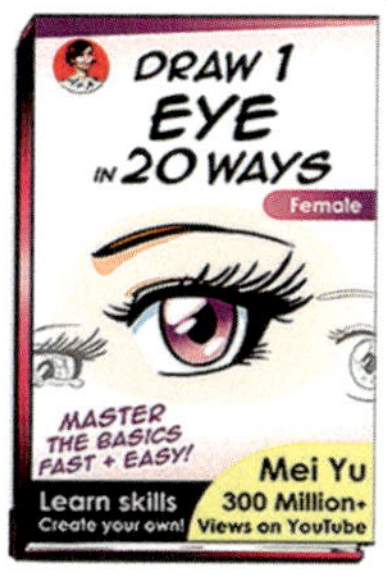

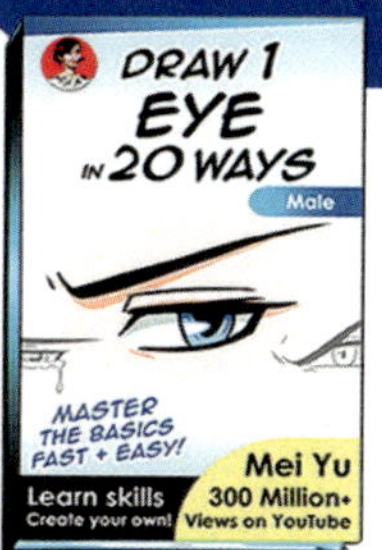

AND MORE...

★ Draw Reimagined Characters Series

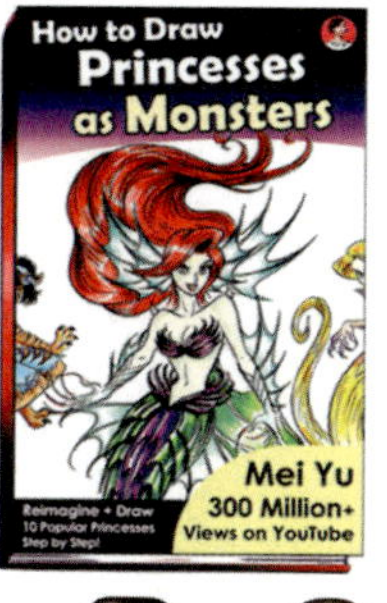

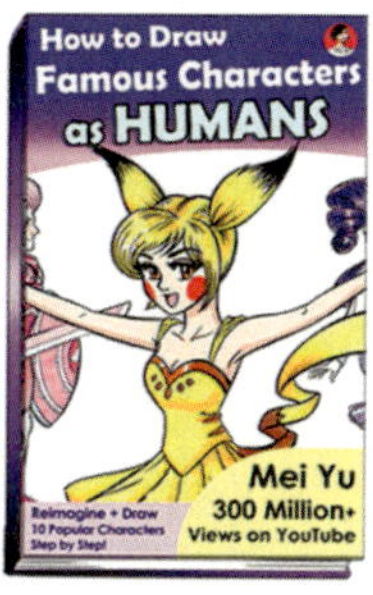

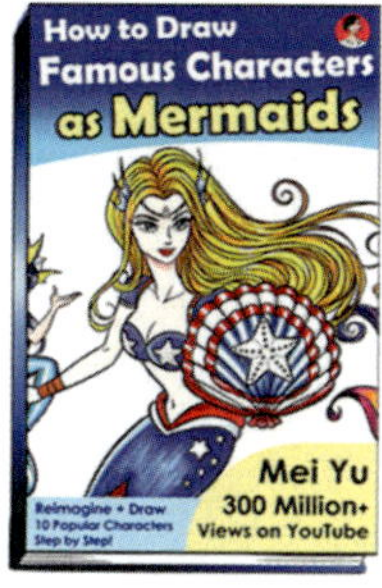

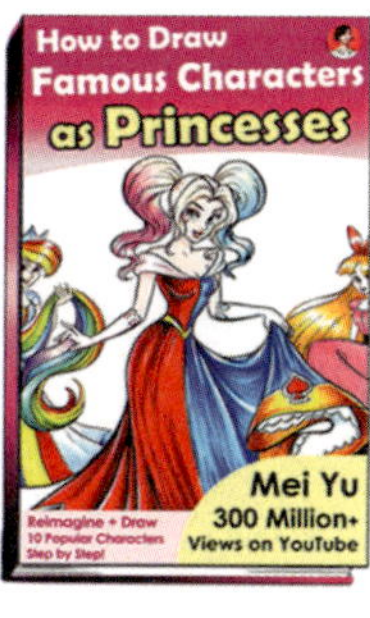

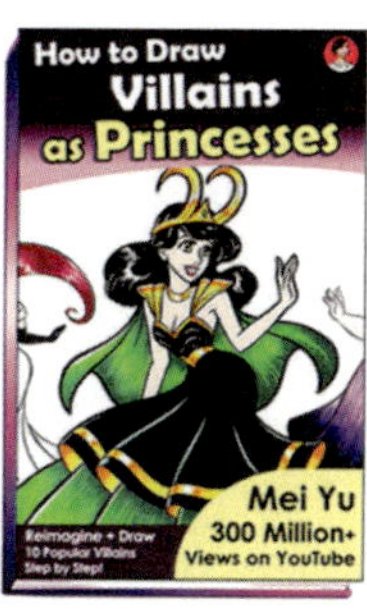

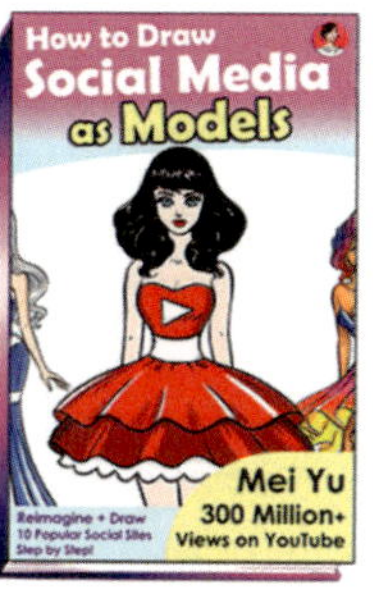

AND MORE...

★ 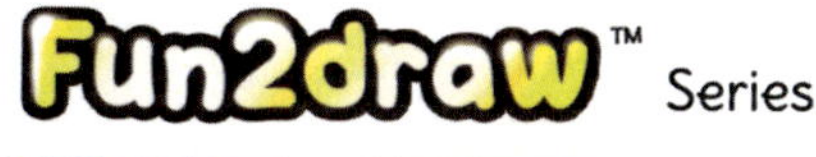 Series

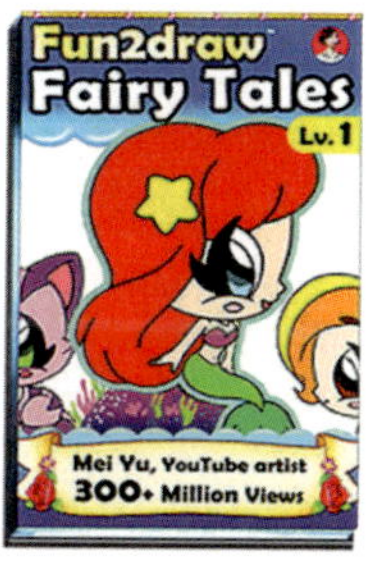

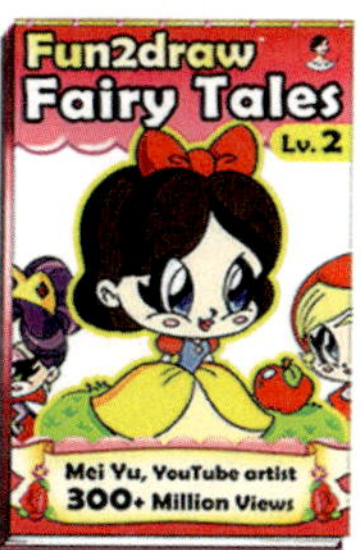

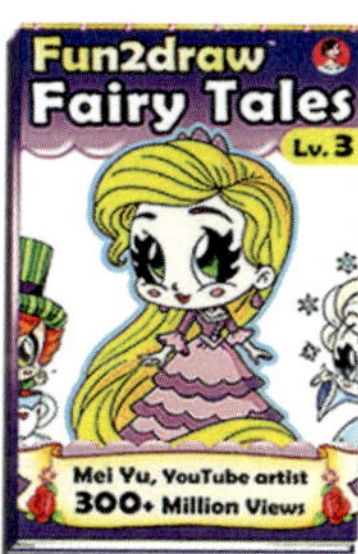

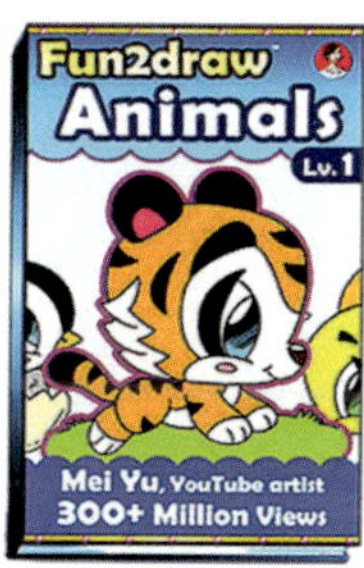

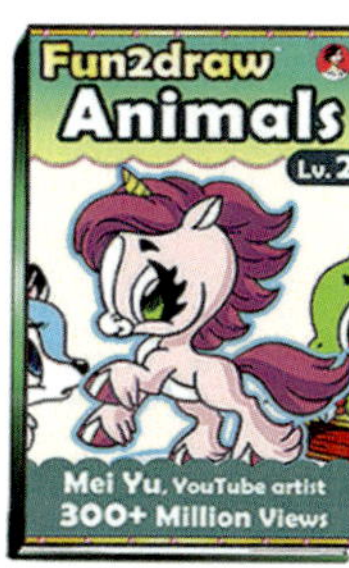

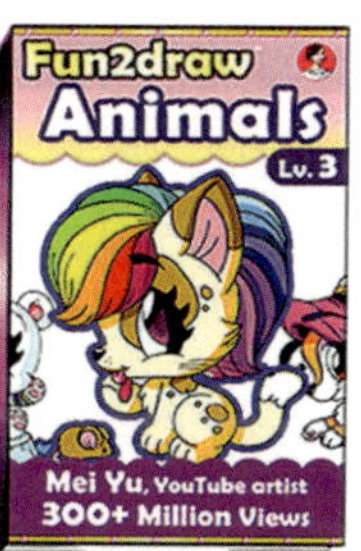

AND MORE...

https://itunes.apple.com/us/author/mei-yu/id1055789735

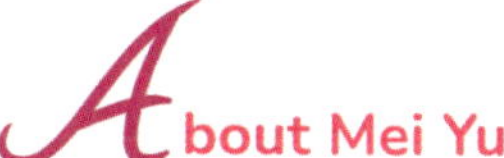

https://www.amazon.com/shop/meiyu

Mei Yu Art

Search Amazon, Kindle, iTunes, Kobo

Android™ users: Download the Kindle App to get my eBooks

Kobo users: Search "Mei Yu Art" in the Kobo app or Kobo website

About Mei Yu

Mei Yu started drawing on walls at age 2. She is a diverse artist and designer from Canada. Mei also has a popular YouTube art channel **www.youtube.com/MeiYu** with over 1.5 million subscribers, 800 videos, and 350 million views.

Mei is happy to know that many fans are inspired by her art and books, and that they are encouraged to pursue art.

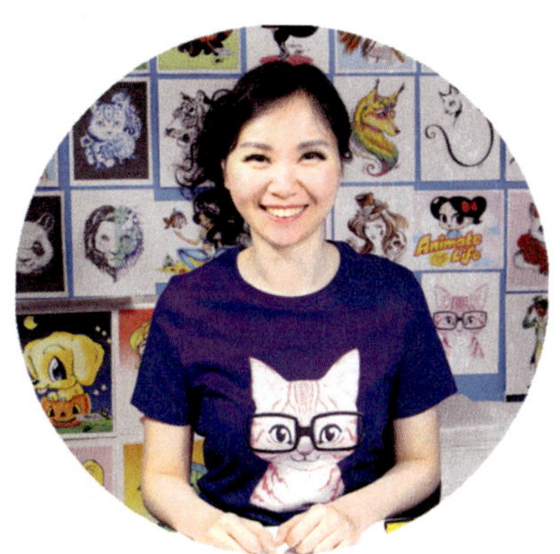

Made in the USA
Monee, IL
29 November 2022

18871577R00026